NARUTO

INNOCENT HEART, DEMONIC BLOOD

INNOCENT HEART, DEMONIC BLOOD

Original Concept by
Masashi Kishimoto

Written by
Masatoshi Kusakabe

Translated by
Tomo Kimura with Janet Gilbert

VIZ Media

San Francisco

Published by
VIZ Media, LLC
295 Bay Street
San Francisco, CA 94133

www.viz.com

Library of Congress Cataloging-in-Publication Data .

Kishimoto, Masashi, 1974-
[Naruto- shiro no dōji, keppū no kijin. English]
Naruto- innocent heart, demonic blood / original concept by Masashi Kishimoto ;
written by Masatoshi Kusakabe ; translated by Tomo Kimura with Janet Gilbert.
p. cm.
ISBN-13: 978-1-4215-0603-6 (pbk : alk. paper)
I. Kusakabe, Masatoshi, 1964- . II. Kimura, Tomo. III. Gilbert, Janet. IV. Title.
PN6790.J34N3713 2006
741.5'952--dc22

                                                              2006023088
Printed in the U.S.A.

First printing, November 2006

CONTENTS

PROFILES

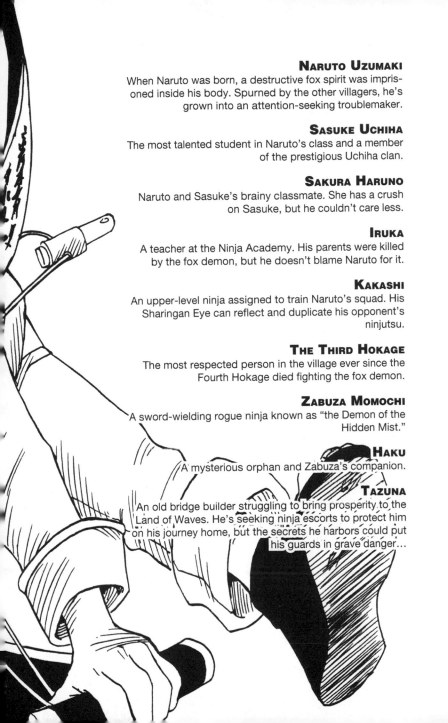

NARUTO UZUMAKI

When Naruto was born, a destructive fox spirit was imprisoned inside his body. Spurned by the other villagers, he's grown into an attention-seeking troublemaker.

SASUKE UCHIHA

The most talented student in Naruto's class and a member of the prestigious Uchiha clan.

SAKURA HARUNO

Naruto and Sasuke's brainy classmate. She has a crush on Sasuke, but he couldn't care less.

IRUKA

A teacher at the Ninja Academy. His parents were killed by the fox demon, but he doesn't blame Naruto for it.

KAKASHI

An upper-level ninja assigned to train Naruto's squad. His Sharingan Eye can reflect and duplicate his opponent's ninjutsu.

THE THIRD HOKAGE

The most respected person in the village ever since the Fourth Hokage died fighting the fox demon.

ZABUZA MOMOCHI

A sword-wielding rogue ninja known as "the Demon of the Hidden Mist."

HAKU

A mysterious orphan and Zabuza's companion.

TAZUNA

An old bridge builder struggling to bring prosperity to the Land of Waves. He's seeking ninja escorts to protect him on his journey home, but the secrets he harbors could put his guards in grave danger…

THE BEGINNING

The beast was humongous.

Whenever it howled, the land shook.

Its nine whirling tails churned up thunder that tore the skies. Razor-sharp claws ripped right through flesh and bone. Long pointed fangs easily chewed up the toughest enemy.

Even its eyes were deadly. One piercing glance from them could turn strong men into stone.

The Nine-Tailed Fox was a spirit that lived in this land. It was as powerful as a demon, or so people said.

Why did the creature attack this peaceful place? Nobody really knew. But the Hidden Leaf Village was definitely in danger.

The Fox howled again.

"Gaa-ooooooooooooo!!!!"

The land shook even harder. The trees in the forest flopped over like little flowers. Black clouds swirled out of nowhere, crackling with lightning.

The Ninja of the Leaves nervously watched from a distance. They were all well trained and ready for combat, but the beast still terrified them.

The ninja knew they could never kill the Fox. But they decided to give it their best shot anyway.

They raised a battle cry to bolster their courage. Then the front line attacked.

The Fox just squinted at them at first. Then it roared, shattering their best secret jutsu into useless little bits. The red-hot flames of a Fire Jutsu vanished into thin air. Ninja were torn to shreds and scattered across the ground.

The others didn't run away, but quickly fired up their own best secret jutsu.

This second attack hit the target. The Fox scowled as fireballs exploded in its face and daggers of stone stabbed its stomach. Shuriken after shuriken whirled through the air as the battle raged on and on.

The shinobi who had been called here to fight were all considered masters. Each one had made a direct hit that he felt sure was a deathblow. They all figured the creature must be hurt, at least a little.

But when the Fox emerged from a cloud of smoke, the ninja all froze in shock. The beast looked exactly the same! Not one small scratch had scarred its hide. It just purred like a kitten, mocking the little people below.

Suddenly the Fox slid forward, too fast for anyone to

see. It slammed into the ninja who were about to release jutsu, and tore them apart with its claws.

The front line survivors, who had retreated after their attack, somehow dodged the blows. But their best secret jutsu were useless against the creature.

They didn't even slow the Fox down!

The Ninja of the Leaves fought on. Shinobi were knocked down, smashed up, and blown away, but the rest kept on going.

They refused to give up. If they did, the Hidden Leaf Village and everything around it would be flattened to the ground.

Soon only a few shinobi were still alive, though just barely. The survivors had no strength left. But their fierce desire to protect their loved ones, plus their well-honed ninja instincts, kept their bodies in motion.

They knew one thing for sure: if the battle continued, they would all die.

Then something happened that no one could have predicted. The Nine-Tailed Fox suddenly swung its head in a different direction.

It was what the Ninja of the Leaves had been hoping for.

A gigantic toad hopped over their tired bodies and landed on the other side of the Fox. As toads go, this one was quite peculiar: it wore a dagger in its belt and a big haori half-coat. A tobacco pipe dangled from its mouth.

The toad bellowed at the Fox in a voice like bubbling mud. The Fox roared back in reply and swung around to face its new enemy.

The two big beasts smashed into each other. The land shook yet again. The toad aimed its dagger and lunged at the Fox, who knocked the weapon away with its chin.

Up to this point, the monsters seemed evenly matched. Then the Fox brought out its deadliest weapon. Soon every one of its nine tails started to thrash at the defenseless toad.

The toad somehow managed to dodge every blow before it vanished in a cloud of smoke.

The Fox looked bewildered. It didn't even notice when a man approached, carrying a small bundle wrapped in a blanket. Without warning, he quickly made a complicated sign and shouted something.

"What is he doing?" the ninja wondered. Then they heard a blood-curdling cry.

What? Could it be? Was the Nine-Tailed Fox... screaming?

It was true! The Nine-Tailed Fox, the king of the spirits, was screaming in pain. This was unheard of!

The Ninja of the Leaves gaped in astonishment as a soft glowing light rose up from the Fox. All of a sudden, the light zoomed toward the man and entered the small bundle in his arms. The whole thing happened in a flash, but for the ninja, the moment felt like forever.

The Nine-Tailed Fox, which hundreds of shinobi couldn't hurt, slowly crumpled to the ground. The infamous nine tails, which had once crushed mountains into pebbles, listlessly flopped around its body.

The earth shook one last time as the dead Fox sunk into the dirt. The ninja rushed forward, shouting with joy...

Then they saw him. His arms and legs were flung out to each side, like a marionette with its strings cut. The man who had stood so bravely against the Fox now lay dead beside his enemy.

He was the Fourth Hokage of the Hidden Leaf Village, the best and strongest shinobi of them all. The healers tried to revive him, but not even the best secret jutsu could bring their leader back to life.

Their joy instantly turned to sorrow. Too stunned to even speak, every shinobi said a silent prayer.

Then it happened.

"Look!" someone shouted, pointing above them.

The small bundle floated down from the sky, glowing with the radiance of all the chakra it held within.

From the center of the bundle came a loud wail. The ninja hurried to unwrap the blanket. Inside was a squirming baby with blond hair.

That baby's name was Naruto.

MEET NARUTO UZUMAKI

"Naruto! Where's Naruto Uzumaki?" Master Iruka shouted as he hurried down a hall inside the Hidden Leaf Village Ninja Academy. His hair was pulled into a ponytail, and an old scar crossed his face near the middle of his nose.

"I have a really bad feeling about this! And right before graduation exams, too," he worried.

Suddenly Iruka heard a loud ruckus outside.

"Look! Look at the Faces!" somebody screamed.

The Great Stone Faces were on a cliff at the edge of the village. The head of every Hokage in history had been carved there. Hokage were the village chiefs and the strongest shinobi of all. Besides the Third, who was still alive, every previous Hokage had given his life to serve the village, so the monument was considered very holy ground.

Iruka's sinking feeling sunk even lower. He dashed out of the academy and climbed to the roof of a nearby building for a bird's-eye view of the Faces.

"What the heck?"

Red blood gushed from every delicately carved nostril. Or was that supposed to be snot?

The First Hokage had a nasty swirl scrawled on his left cheek, while a steaming pile of poop decorated the Third Hokage's right cheek. More graffiti was scribbled everywhere.

"Narutooooo!"

Iruka clenched his fists, gritted his teeth, and took off running.

A kid in an orange jumpsuit hung by a rope in front of the monument. His blond hair poked up in jagged tufts, as if it had been hacked at with a sword. He wore goggles on his forehead and a huge grin on his face.

No one else was smiling. The villagers just shook their heads as they watched him from below.

Naruto Uzumaki was small compared to other kids his age, but he handled the rope deftly as he drew with a big brush.

"Hee hee! This next one will really get 'em!" Naruto snorted, dipping his brush in the paint. He was about to create another masterpiece when he heard an angry voice from the crowd.

"Hey, you! Cut it out! All you ever do is pull pranks!" a chunin yelled.

"Aw, shut up!" Naruto sneered down at him. "You guys

would never even think of doin' something like this!"

Naruto was right. Nobody would dare to doodle on the Great Stone Faces. The monument was sacred to the villagers, something they weren't even supposed to touch.

Which made it the perfect place for Naruto's latest crime spree. He'd had a hard time making mischief lately, since most of the villagers were completely on their guard around him.

"Check it out, people! I win as usual!" Naruto bragged.

Just then the Third Hokage joined the spectators. He was the village's most important man, but Naruto actually liked him. True, they hadn't spoken much, but there was something about him that interested Naruto, something different from the other adults.

The Hokage had a sour look, but he didn't seem all that angry. He just stood there, watching the show, until a shadow crossed his path.

"I apologize, Lord Hokage. It's all my fault," the shadow said nervously.

"Ah! Iruka," the Hokage said, turning to him.

"Uh-oh! <u>Sensei's</u> here!" Naruto gasped. He suddenly lost his balance and clung to the rope for dear life. Too late! With a pitiful scream, Naruto fell off the Great Stone Faces, clutching his tattered rope.

Iruka covered his face with his hands and sighed.

"What does he think he's doing? The graduation exam

is tomorrow!" he muttered to himself.

Luckily, a tree branch caught Naruto on his way down. Iruka lassoed him with a rope and dragged him back to school.

Iruka's classroom had stadium-style seating, with several tiers rising from the teacher's podium. Naruto felt cold eyes glare down from every corner as Iruka royally chewed him out.

"You've flunked the exam twice already, Naruto! You should not be fooling around like that!" Iruka scolded.

"Yeah, yeah. Whatever," Naruto mumbled, too scared to make eye contact.

Iruka grunted and turned to the rest of class.

"Line up, people! Time for a pop quiz!" he said firmly.

The class booed in unison. Iruka totally ignored them.

"Today you will do the Transformation Jutsu. You will transform to look exactly like me. Now line up, I said!"

The students staggered to their feet and reluctantly formed a line. Every pair of eyes shot daggers at Naruto.

"This is all your fault!"

"What's with you, anyway?"

Naruto sat down and refused to budge.

"Naruto! Get in line!" Iruka barked, unwinding the lasso. Naruto got up and went to the back, sulking all the while.

The Transformation Jutsu isn't really that difficult. With a little practice, almost anyone can transform themselves.

18

Fighting or using another jutsu while transformed is another story. But a simple, no-frills transformation? Easy-peasy.

Even Naruto had the ability, or at least he should have. When his turn came, he stepped in front of Iruka and made the Transformation Jutsu hand sign.

All of a sudden Iruka felt something bad was about to happen. Naruto was acting as innocent as a newborn babe, but his eyes told a different story.

"Transform!" Naruto yelled.

He cloaked himself in smoke while Iruka watched with anxiety. Soon a vision emerged from behind the dark cloud.

"I call it Sexy Jutsu!" Naruto said with pride.

A completely naked girl, like a model from one of *those* magazines, was posing prettily on one leg. The weird thing was, Iruka thought he recognized her.

Iruka felt hot liquid in his nose and cupped his hand under his nostrils. His palm instantly brimmed over with bright red blood.

"Hey, baby!" the naked girl said in Naruto's voice. She struck another sexy pose. Iruka's nosebleed gushed forth with fury. His consciousness was waning fast.

"Ain't she cool?" Naruto sniggered.

Just hearing Naruto's voice brought Iruka back to earth again. He jumped up and instantly went on the warpath.

"You fool! Don't invent stupid jutsu like that!" Iruka roared, jerking Naruto away by his collar.

"But, sensei! What about the quiz?" someone asked.

Iruka swung back to look at his students.

"We're done for today, people," he snapped. "Study on your own until the end of class!"

"Yay! We get to study on our own!"

Iruka dragged Naruto down the hall, out the door, and all the way back to the Great Stone Faces.

"You are not going home until you clean up that mess," Iruka said angrily.

Soon Naruto was standing on a foothold, scrubbing off doodles with a cold wet rag. Every so often, he paused to glance at Iruka. Then he kept on scrubbing.

Iruka sighed.

Why is he like this? he asked himself for the millionth time. Iruka was deep in thought until he heard some grumbling from above.

"So what if I can't go home? No one's waiting there for me anyway," Naruto muttered.

Iruka felt a cold blade pierce his heart. Naruto was right. He was all alone. The Hokage and others secretly took care of him, did their duty. But they didn't act out of love. They took care of Naruto because they were afraid the tortured spirit sealed inside him might break out someday. They were afraid of the Nine-Tailed Fox.

Naruto's parents had both died right after he was born. The little blond boy had been mostly by himself since he was a toddler. He had never known any special affection from someone close to him. No wonder he craved attention.

Why didn't I realize this before? Iruka anguished, beating himself up inside. Naruto's in the same boat that I was.

"Uh, Naruto? When you're all done..." Iruka began.

"Then what?" Naruto groaned. His arms were killing him.

Iruka looked up sheepishly.

"When you're all done, I'll buy you a bowl of ramen."

"All right!" Naruto yelled. He looked ready to leave right then. Iruka smiled despite himself.

"But only if you clean up everything!" he reminded Naruto.

"I will! I will!" Naruto promised.

When Naruto finally finished, it was already dark. The two ambled over to Ichiraku Ramen, the all-time favorite of ninja academy students. Naruto was really, really tired after all that hard labor, so he was really, really hungry. He attacked his ramen with wild abandon.

"You know, Ichiraku's ramen really is the best," Naruto said between slurps. In truth, Naruto had never met a noodle he didn't love. He was hopelessly addicted to them.

Iruka watched Naruto greedily gobble his supper for a while. Finally, he spoke.

"Why did you do it, Naruto? You know how much the villagers respect the Hokage."

Naruto looked up with surprise.

"Of course I know!" he spit out, his mouth crammed

with ramen. He took a big swallow and smiled.

"People who earn the title of Hokage are the best ninja in the village," Naruto said earnestly. "Don't forget, the Fourth Hokage rescued the village from the Demon Fox."

"So you do understand. But you still haven't told me why you did it," Iruka said.

"Because someday my face will be up there," Naruto declared, his eyes shining. "And I'll be better than any of them! The entire village will respect me and my powers!"

"So you want to be a Hokage," Iruka murmured, feeling uncomfortable all of a sudden.

What in the world should he say now? Should he encourage Naruto's impossible dream? Or should he just keep his trap shut? While Iruka weighed the options, Naruto chuckled nervously.

"Um, sensei? Can I ask you a favor?" he said.

Iruka looked him in the eye. *Now what?* he thought.

"Pleeeease let me wear your headband! Just for a little while!" Naruto begged.

Ninja wore headbands for protection, but Naruto didn't care about that. To him, a headband shouted to the world, "Look at me, everybody! I'm a ninja!"

"Nope," Iruka said flatly. "If you want to wear one so badly, pass the exam tomorrow. Then you'll earn your own."

"Tsk! Pretty selfish for a teacher," Naruto pouted.

He bent over his bowl and shoveled in the rest of the ramen. Those poor wet noodles never had a fighting chance. When he finished, Naruto licked his lips and came up for air.

"I'll take seconds," he said without batting an eye.

"Now who's the selfish one? I never promised you two bowls of ramen!" Iruka snarled.

In the end, Naruto ate three, count 'em, three huge helpings. Iruka paid for every bowl.

They left Ichiraku and went off in different directions.

"See you tomorrow, sensei!" Naruto shouted. He turned back and waved before he started running toward home. Iruka watched until Naruto was out of sight. Then he sighed. Just how should he handle him now?

The next day, the graduation exam began.

"You will all do the Clone Jutsu first," Iruka told the

class before he left for the exam room. Names would be called in order, one by one. Each student would be tested alone.

At the back of the classroom, Naruto shuddered. The Clone Jutsu always gave him trouble. In theory, it was a lot like the Transformation Jutsu, only instead of making yourself into something else, you made yourself into yourself, over and over again. But that tiny difference seemed enormous to Naruto.

Soon his name was called.

"Showtime," he muttered, hurrying to the exam room.

Iruka and a sensei named Mizuki sat at a table in the back of the room. Naruto didn't know Mizuki well, but he had a pretty good feeling about him. Mizuki had never shunned him like all the other teachers—all the other teachers except Iruka, that is.

Naruto swallowed hard. The prized Leaf headbands were spread out on the table where the teachers sat. They looked absolutely beautiful.

"Naruto Uzumaki, begin," Iruka said in a serious tone.

Naruto made the correct hand sign. Then, concentrating with all his might, he did the required jutsu.

"Clone Jutsu!" Naruto cried when he finished.

The thick-as-pea-soup smoke particular to ninjutsu rose. Naruto looked around for his clone. When he saw it, he gasped.

It was him, all right. But this clone looked sick, like he hadn't slept for a week! He was passed out limply on the floor, showing just the whites of his eyes.

"Naruto Uzumaki, you fail," Iruka boomed out. Naruto just stood looking at his feet. He didn't even have the heart to mouth off. He was about to leave when Mizuki spoke.

"Iruka-sensei, I think you could pass him," Mizuki reasoned. "He did make a clone, after all. And a unique jutsu like that isn't easy."

Naruto looked up hopefully.

"We can't do that," Iruka said gruffly. "The other students all made at least three clones. Naruto made just one, and a useless one at that. We can't let him pass."

"Aw, c'mon!" Naruto pleaded. Iruka glared at him.

"Other students are waiting, Naruto. Goodbye."

Naruto walked out of the room with his head down and his mind completely blank.

Outside the school, students who had passed the exam were happily celebrating with their parents. Naruto didn't want to be near them, but he didn't feel like leaving, either. So he went to the edge of the schoolyard and plopped down on a swing. He pumped his legs fast and furiously until he was soon riding high.

"Oh! That's him, isn't it?" he heard a mother hiss in his direction.

"Yep, that's him," another mother hissed back. "I guess he flunked."

"Good. Someone like him can't become a ninja! Think of what might happen!"

"I know! If his true nature ever emerges, we'll all be—"

But before they could go on, a third mother quickly interrupted them.

"Shhhh, you two! We're not supposed to talk about him, remember?" she chided.

Naruto had heard more than enough. He jumped off the swing and trudged away with his head down. Where should he go now? There was no place in this village where he truly felt welcome.

"Iruka-sensei is a jerk!" Naruto grumbled to the ground. "A doofus! A big fat son of a—"

"Hello, Naruto," a kind voice said. Naruto yanked up his head. Mizuki stood in front of him, smiling with sympathy.

"C'mon, let's get out of here," he said.

Soon they were sitting on the balcony of a tall building nearby, enjoying a panoramic view of the town. The villagers rarely came here, but Naruto was glad Mizuki had suggested it.

They sat in silence for a while, until Mizuki finally spoke.

"Don't hate him, Naruto," he said.

"Who?"

"Iruka-sensei. He lost his parents when he was very small, so he's been alone most of his life. Going through all that has made him a very serious man."

"Pfft! So why does he keep picking on me?" Naruto griped, puffing out his cheeks.

"He thinks you're like him."

"Like him? How?" Naruto asked with surprise.

"You don't have parents either," Mizuki explained. "Iruka wants you to become as strong as he's had to be. Can you at least try to understand?"

Naruto frowned and stared straight ahead.

"But I wanted to graduate," he muttered.

Mizuki gave Naruto a quick, sharp look. Then his face softened to its usual mild expression.

"You want to graduate? Then do something to impress Iruka-sensei," he suggested gently.

"Like what?"

"I have an idea. Do this, and he will definitely be happy."

"Wh-what is it?" Naruto asked nervously.

Mizuki glanced around to see if anyone was listening. Then he whispered in Naruto's ear.

Naruto suddenly grinned. He grinned so wide that people the next land over probably saw all his teeth, if they happened to be looking, that is.

The Third Hokage was very old, but he wasn't feeble. In fact, most of his skills were still as sharp as shuriken points.

So it was no surprise that late one night, while he was writing in his journal, he heard someone sneak up to his house.

The Third Hokage lowered his eyelids and focused his attention on the intruder. No evil vibes there. This stranger was not about to murder him. Judging from his size, he was either a very small man or a child.

"Naruto? Is that you?" the Hokage called out.

Sometimes Konohamaru, his grandson, played tricks like this, but Konohamaru would be fast asleep at this hour. The Hokage sharpened his focus until he was sure of the intruder's identity. Then he heaved a big sigh.

"Now what is he scheming?" he muttered.

The Hokage moved closer, until he could sense Naruto's energy. All of a sudden he saw him. Naruto had crawled through a window and was now tiptoeing toward the back of the house.

"What are you doing here?" the Hokage barked.

Naruto squealed and wildly spun around.

He gaped at the Third Hokage for exactly three seconds. Then he quickly made a hand sign and shouted, "Sexy Jutsu!"

Now the Third Hokage was very gifted. He knew more secret jutsu than any Hokage before him, and could execute that secret jutsu better than anybody. Make no mistake, the Third Hokage was truly a living legend.

But even living legends have weak spots. The last time

the Third Hokage had seen a woman, make that a young woman, in all her lush, glorious splendor was ages and ages ago.

By sheer accident, Naruto had discovered the Hokage's one niggling little weakness—and had exploited the living heck out of it.

Amazing how nosebleeds can spurt out so spectacularly, the Hokage thought, slowly sinking into oblivion.

"Close one," Naruto gulped, rushing away. He tore through the mansion until he found the library Mizuki had told him about. The shelves were jam-packed with scrolls, but Naruto didn't stop to browse. He headed straight for a corner that was away from the other books.

"This must be it," he said out loud.

Naruto pulled out a scroll as long as his arm and quickly scanned its contents. Bingo. He rolled it back up, tucked it under his arm, and crawled out a nearby window.

A shadow, hidden from view, had been watching the entire operation. Naruto never noticed.

They didn't find the Third Hokage until early the next morning. He was still unconscious, eyes rolled back, blood gushing from his nose. The walls, ceiling, and floor were all spattered with big red blobs.

That same night, in another house, Iruka tossed and turned. He couldn't stop agonizing about Naruto's fate. What should he do about him? What could he do?

To make matters worse, the Third Hokage had called on Iruka after the exam with a surprising request.

"I understand your position on this, but Naruto needs your affection, too," the Hokage had told him.

"Affection?"

"I'm not saying you shouldn't scold him," the Hokage continued. "Naruto needs a firm hand. But he also needs love. Someone who treats him tenderly, like a parent. Please remember that."

Iruka knew the Hokage was right. He had felt guilty as all get-out for snapping at Naruto after the test.

But some dark feeling inside Iruka kept him from truly opening his heart. He didn't hate Naruto, but he knew they could never be close. Iruka obsessed about all this until dawn, when someone started banging on his door.

"Who can it be at this hour?" he said, feeling irritated.

"Iruka! Please hurry!" Mizuki burst out when Iruka opened the door.

"What happened?" Iruka gasped.

"We think Naruto stole the Scroll of Sealing. Come to Lord Hokage's mansion with me."

"Naruto did what?"

Mizuki didn't answer, but ran off into the morning light. Iruka ran off after him. By the time they arrived at the mansion, the chief chunin were already there.

"You're late, Iruka," the Third Hokage said sternly.

"Sorry, Lord Hokage."

The Third Hokage nodded and cleared his throat.

"As you've all heard, the Scroll of Sealing is missing," he said gravely. "We think it was taken some hours ago. If we don't find the scroll soon, there will be dire consequences."

The Scroll of Sealing contained dangerous special jutsu compiled by the First Hokage years ago. Like any important reference book, it was never allowed out of the library. Only Hokage were allowed to look inside, but they had never shared its secrets.

"This is more than a childish prank," the Hokage went on.

A chunin named Bekko looked grim. So did the others. Mizuki looked sad, but he didn't object to punishing Naruto when they found him—if they found him.

"Our first priority is to get that scroll," the Hokage directed. "We can decide about Naruto later. Go!"

The chunin scattered in all directions.

As Iruka jumped from roof to roof, he vowed to be first to find Naruto.

He had to be first. There was no telling what the others might do if they caught Naruto red-handed. Besides, Iruka was dying to discover how Naruto had found out about the scroll. Naruto wasn't supposed to know that it even existed.

"I have a sneaking suspicion where he might be," Iruka muttered. "But I'll turn over every stone in the village until

I find him."

Suddenly Iruka had another sneaking suspicion. Was someone lurking behind his back?

Iruka didn't have time to investigate. He took off for the first place on his list.

FRIENDS—OR ENEMIES?

Meanwhile, in the middle of the forest, Naruto sat on the ground in a daze. He'd been practicing a special jutsu since daybreak. Now every bone in his body ached.

Mizuki had told him the truth, all right. Every jutsu in the Scroll of Sealing was totally amazing. Only trouble was, Naruto couldn't figure out most of them.

He wound up choosing a jutsu that seemed sort of easy, at least compared to the others. But even the scroll's easiest jutsu made the Clone Jutsu look like child's play.

Naruto went through the motions again and again, trying hard to get them right. Now, hours later, he was actually making progress.

"I just need more practice," Naruto told himself.

He tried to stand up, but his legs felt as limp as leftover ramen. Naruto was so focused on getting to his feet that he didn't hear someone approach.

"Narutoooo!"

Naruto blinked his bleary eyes in the direction of the voice. Then he grinned.

"Hey, sensei! I found you!" Naruto yelled.

"I found you, fool!" Iruka yelled back.

Naruto wobbled to his feet, and Iruka gasped with surprise.

"What are you doing out here? You look dead tired."

"I am dead tired," Naruto admitted. "I've been practicing ninjutsu."

"You have?"

Iruka suddenly looked uneasy.

"Here, I'll show you!" Naruto said excitedly, getting into position. "If I do this, you'll have to let me graduate!"

Shoot, if I do this, they'll promote me all the way to a chunin, Naruto thought wildly as he made the complicated signs.

"Not so fast, Naruto," Iruka blurted. "What's that scroll on your back?"

The scroll was as big and heavy as a log, but Naruto had forgotten all about it.

"This old thing? Mizuki-sensei said I could graduate if I learned a jutsu from this scroll. So I borrowed it from Grandpa Hokage."

"Mizuki told you about the scroll?" Iruka gasped.

Without warning, he roughly pushed Naruto aside. Naruto fell backward as a storm of shuriken spun right toward Iruka.

Iruka felt them pierce every part of his body. He staggered around in pain, struggling to keep on his feet.

"S-sensei?" Naruto said uneasily. Iruka glared up at a nearby tree.

"Hello, Mizuki. So you were the one stalking me," he said grimly.

Mizuki stood on a branch near the top of a tree. Several huge windmill shuriken were strapped to his back.

"I thought you might lead me to Naruto," Mizuki said, descending from his lofty perch.

"I see."

Iruka plucked a shuriken from his arm and grimaced. Naruto watched the two sensei with confusion.

"Wh-what's going on?" he stuttered.

"Give me the scroll, Naruto," Mizuki said coldly.

Naruto had never seen Mizuki look so menacing, his mouth twisted into a nasty smile.

"Don't, Naruto! No matter what he says!" Iruka hollered. "That scroll contains dangerous jutsu! Mizuki tricked you into stealing the scroll so he could get it for himself!"

Naruto gaped at Mizuki with shock and quickly struck a fighting pose.

"You don't need that scroll, Naruto! Just give it to me!" Mizuki demanded.

"N-no," Naruto stammered.

"Why? Because Iruka-sensei said not to?" Mizuki

scoffed. "Would you like to know what Iruka-sensei really thinks of you?"

Iruka suddenly looked horrified.

"No, Mizuki! Don't do this!" he cried.

Mizuki ignored him and turned toward Naruto.

"Do you know who killed Iruka's parents?" he began.

"Uh, the fox demon, right? That thing with the nine tails," Naruto said.

Mizuki snorted with amusement.

"A brilliant answer, Naruto. Especially coming from you."

"I said stop!" Iruka yelled, lunging at Mizuki. But the shuriken had done their damage. Iruka fell painfully to his knees.

"A brilliant answer, yet not quite accurate," Mizuki continued.

"Stop!" Iruka yelled again, but Mizuki went on.

"Think hard about my question, Naruto. I asked you who killed Iruka's parents, not what."

"Who?" Naruto asked, puzzled. "You make it sound almost human."

"Because it is, Naruto! The Nine-Tailed Fox has changed its form, but it's still alive."

"That's enough, Mizuki!" Iruka screamed.

Mizuki leaned forward and got right in Naruto's face.

"The Fourth Hokage didn't kill the Nine-Tailed Fox. He just sucked out its spirit and sealed it inside a human," he said. "Ever since, our village has had one strict decree: that human's identity must never be revealed."

"Wh-what decree? I never heard about it," Naruto said nervously.

Naruto was telling the truth. He knew about other village decrees, had even broken a few just for fun. But nobody had ever mentioned that particular one.

"Of course you don't know," Mizuki snapped. "But it's high time you did."

"Noooooo..." Iruka moaned. He pulled a shuriken from his thigh and made a wild throw. Mizuki dodged it without effort.

"Naruto, the human with the spirit of the Nine-Tailed Fox inside is...you."

"Wh-what do you mean?" Naruto choked.

"You killed Iruka's parents and wiped out the whole village!" Mizuki snarled.

Darkness seemed to descend over everything.

"Ever wonder why the villagers shun you? Gossip about you? Treat you like absolute dirt?"

"N-no!" Naruto shouted, his small body shaking with anger.

"Don't listen to him, Naruto! He's not telling the—"

"Truth, Iruka? The truth is, you hate the Nine-Tailed Fox more than anybody," Mizuki sneered.

Naruto looked at Iruka's face with pleading eyes.

"No, Naruto. That's not—" Iruka started to say.

Mizuki pulled one of the massive shuriken from his back.

"Even Iruka hates you, Naruto! You killed his parents! No one can stand the sight of you!"

The big shuriken buzzed in Mizuki's hands, but Naruto was too upset to notice.

"Noooooo!" Naruto bellowed.

He looked ready to explode with rage. Iruka had never seen Naruto get so angry before. It absolutely terrified him.

"You did your job, Naruto! Die in peace!" Mizuki roared.

Naruto froze as the giant shuriken spun toward him. He didn't scream, or tremble, or even shed a tear. He just stood there, absolutely stunned.

Everything went black as Naruto fell backward. Then a strange thing happened. Suddenly his whole body felt cradled by something soft and warm.

Naruto looked up to find himself in Iruka's arms.

"S-sensei?" he said weakly.

Iruka slowly pulled away. Naruto shuddered when he saw the huge shuriken sticking out of Iruka's back. Iruka's heavy jacket had softened the blow somewhat, but he was still seriously injured.

Iruka looked at Naruto and burst into tears.

"You must have felt so lonely, Naruto," Iruka sobbed. "You must have suffered so much."

Naruto gaped at Iruka in utter astonishment.

Tears rolled down Iruka's cheeks as he remembered what the Hokage had said.

Naruto needs a firm hand. But he also needs love.

That need felt all too familiar to Iruka. He had also longed for someone to love him after his parents died.

As a boy, Iruka had even pulled a few pranks to get noticed, though never as many as Naruto. He just wanted somebody, anybody to acknowledge he even existed.

Naruto is me, Iruka thought. *No wonder I could never get close to him.*

But for some reason, Iruka felt different now. He had thrown himself in the shuriken's path without a second thought, and that one brave move had cracked his heart wide open. Now Naruto was his dear student, someone he had to protect.

Rest assured, Iruka would still scream bloody murder whenever Naruto wreaked havoc. Only now Iruka would understand why Naruto did what he did. At long last, Iruka finally knew how to handle him.

But was it already too late?

Iruka coughed and cleared his throat.

"I'm sorry, Naruto. I should have realized what you were going through," Iruka said gently. Blood dripped from the corners of his mouth, a sure sign of internal injuries.

Naruto looked at Iruka with awe. Then he jumped up and ran into the forest with the scroll.

"Poor, poor Iruka. Looks like your sob story fell on deaf ears."

Iruka sensed Mizuki behind him.

"He'll get revenge on the village with that scroll, you know," Mizuki continued. "Did you see the Nine-Tailed Fox in his eyes? Horrifying, to say the least."

Naruto's incredible fury had truly shocked Iruka. But he still had to protect him.

Iruka got up and yanked the shuriken from his back, trying to ignore the searing pain.

"Naruto isn't like that," he told Mizuki.

"Believe whatever you want. I'm getting that scroll," Mizuki snarled as he zoomed away.

"Wait! Mizuki!"

"Just try and catch me, Iruka."

Iruka tottered forward, but his legs quickly buckled under him.

"Not now!" he yelled, kneeling in the dirt. "Move, you dumb things!"

His legs, like his students, finally obeyed, and Iruka dashed off after Mizuki.

SHOWDOWN

The Third Hokage sat in his study, gazing at a crystal ball. Tiny figures of Naruto, Iruka, and Mizuki were reflected inside, like actors on a miniature stage.

He suddenly looked away in disgust.

"They finally find Naruto, and now this happens? What is Mizuki thinking?"

The Hokage believed Naruto was in a very unstable state right now. For twelve years, the Fourth Hokage's seal had held fast. But could it hold forever?

Worse yet, Naruto still had the scroll with that seal's secret jutsu. If the seal broke, and the Nine-Tailed Fox took over Naruto's consciousness, the beast could use that jutsu to resurrect itself.

The Hokage puffed on his pipe. *I should say a prayer,* he thought sadly. Naruto was just a kid, after all—a ramen-loving, prank-pulling, sensei-sassing kid. True, the Nine-Tailed Fox was sealed inside him, but that wasn't Naruto's fault.

"It would be a shame to lose him," the Hokage whispered to himself, shaking out his pipe in an ashtray.

High up in the tree canopy, Naruto leaped from branch to branch, the big scroll still on his back.

"Naruto! There you are!" Iruka yelled when he spotted him. He went up a nearby tree and started moving in tandem with his student.

"Hurry, toss me that scroll! Mizuki's just itching to grab it!"

Naruto glanced at his sensei, but didn't bother to answer. He rapidly changed direction and flew straight at Iruka, who had just leapt off a branch.

They slammed into each other in midair. Iruka lost his balance and crashed to the ground.

With nothing to break his fall, Iruka rolled around in a messy heap. He glared at Naruto, who drifted down as gently as a gingko leaf.

"Why?" Iruka sputtered as a cloud of smoke enveloped him. It soon faded to reveal Mizuki, seething with rage.

"Naruto! How did you know I wasn't Iruka?" Mizuki hollered.

"Because I'm Iruka," Naruto smirked. More smoke went up and soon Iruka appeared, injured but still determined.

Meanwhile, the real Naruto was watching all this from a distance. *What now?* he thought frantically. *Iruka-sensei will die if I don't do something!*

But what should he do? *Help him or you'll be sorry,* shouted a voice inside Naruto. But Mizuki's voice was even louder.

"Why are you protecting the little punk, Iruka?" Mizuki screeched. "He killed your parents! A horrible monster lives inside him!"

"For the last time, Naruto isn't like that," Iruka insisted.

"Pfft! What do you know?" Mizuki scoffed. "Naruto is the same as I am."

"What do you mean?"

Mizuki laughed like a madman.

"The jutsu in the Scroll of Sealing can make all things possible. I could tear the heavens, split the earth, make every star in the sky fall down. Just think of what the Nine-Tailed Fox might do with that knowledge."

"You could be right, Mizuki," Iruka admitted.

Iruka's words wrapped round Naruto's heart like a hangman's noose.

Just as I thought. Nobody really cares about me.

Iruka didn't. Neither did Mizuki. People pretended to care, but in the end they only cared about themselves. That was just how humans were, how they always would be.

Even Iruka-sensei doesn't really accept me, Naruto despaired. The noose tightened. Suddenly Naruto heard another voice, coming from a dark place deep inside him. It was a cruel voice, cackling with triumph.

If you lose yourself, I'll be free again! If you lose yourself, I'll be free again...

A chill shot up Naruto's spine. Then he heard Iruka again.

"You could be right, if Naruto was the Nine-Tailed Fox," he was saying.

Naruto strained to listen as Iruka hoarsely continued.

"But Naruto is actually..."

Iruka paused. Naruto braced himself for the bad news.

"Naruto is actually an excellent student," Iruka concluded.

"Oh, sure he is! A real scholar!" Mizuki jeered.

Iruka ignored him and went on.

"So he's a little clumsy. Big deal! He still works hard, and with very little encouragement from anybody."

Naruto felt a lump in his throat. He clutched the Scroll of Sealing more closely against his chest.

"He's not a fox demon anymore, Mizuki," Iruka beamed. "He's Naruto Uzumaki of the Village Hidden in the Leaves."

Tears trickled down Naruto's face. He had shed many lonely tears on many lonely nights, but these tears were very different.

"Stupid, stupid Iruka," Mizuki sneered, reaching for another big shuriken. "I was going to kill you later, but there's no time like the present!"

Mizuki took aim again at Iruka, who by now could barely move. Iruka stood mesmerized for a moment, then closed his eyes and steeled himself.

This is it, he thought. *Sorry, Naruto. I really wanted to—*

Suddenly Iruka heard a sharp hiss. He opened his eyes just in time to see Naruto kick Mizuki in the butt.

Mizuki was taken by complete surprise. He threw up his hands, which sent the shuriken spinning to the sky. Soon its gruesome blades, which could slice a human in half, lodged into nearby tree trunk.

Mizuki fell smack down on his face. When he slowly picked himself up, his cheeks looked like raw meat.

"You brat! You made a fool of me!" Mizuki screamed, his body quivering with anger.

"Keep your hands off Iruka-sensei, or I'll kill you," Naruto growled in a voice Iruka had never heard before. But for some reason, Naruto's anger didn't scare him this time. Iruka was too busy worrying. Naruto wasn't even a genin yet. How could he possibly defeat a chunin?

"Run, Naruto! Don't worry about me!" Iruka shouted.

"I'll kill you with one punch, you little freak!" Mizuki roared.

"Just try it, scum," Naruto said calmly. "I'll multiply it by a thousand and bounce it back at you."

Naruto's placid demeanor was really getting to Mizuki.

"Bring it on, Nine-Tailed Fox!" he roared.

Suddenly Mizuki froze to the spot. All the blood drained from his face as his eyes darted in every direction.

Naruto was multiplying fast—incredibly fast. First there were ten Narutos, then twenty, and then...

"There's a thousand of them!" Mizuki gagged.

Just yesterday, Naruto had barely managed to make one. Now Naruto clones were popping up everywhere, like worms after a heavy rain.

"Oh, great! Now he can do it!" Mizuki groaned.

"The Shadow Clone Jutsu!" the Narutos shouted in unison.

The regular Clone Jutsu is an example of genjutsu, the art of illusion. Though the clones made with it look real, they are actually just a visual trick.

The Shadow Clone Jutsu, on the other hand, is drastically different. Using his own chakra, a ninja can create clones with actual substance and manipulate them at will. This skill belonged to a higher class of ninjutsu, too difficult for ordinary ninja to master.

Naruto didn't use the Shadow Clone Jutsu, however. He used the Multi-Shadow Clone Jutsu, which is even harder!

"This jutsu was sealed in the scroll," the Narutos said.

Iruka couldn't believe his eyes. He felt shocked and proud and elated, all at same time. Mizuki, however, was just plain shocked.

"What's the holdup, Mizuki?" the thousand Narutos said. "You said you'd kill me with one punch, remember?"

The sight of that many Narutos all talking at once was awe-inspiring indeed. Mizuki could hardly breathe, let alone speak.

"All right, Mizuki," the Narutos said patiently. "If you won't come to me, then I'll come to you."

The gang of Narutos marched toward Mizuki, who cowered like a little baby. Even his best ninjutsu was worthless against this army of spiky-haired boys.

Mizuki was swallowed up in a sea of orange jumpsuits. Soon the sounds of pummeling fists alternated with pitiful pleas for mercy.

Mizuki was pushed back, knocked around, and finally struck down. The thousand Narutos disappeared, leaving behind just the original—and he was grinning from ear to ear. Naruto gazed down at poor Mizuki, who was sprawled on the ground with his face bashed in.

"Uh-oh! Guess I kinda overdid it," Naruto said sheepishly.

"Naruto, come here," Iruka beckoned. He had been sitting on a tree root, watching the whole siege. Naruto suddenly felt scared. Was he in trouble for socking a sensei?

"Uh, I, um..." he mumbled, stalling for time.

"I'm not angry, you fool! I have something for you.

Naruto approached with trepidation, but Iru

smiling at him.

"Close your eyes, Naruto," he said.

"Uh, sensei? Don't do anything weird, okay?"

"I promise. Now don't peek until I say so."

Naruto heard a rustle, then felt something being wrapped around his head.

"Ta-da! You can look now," Iruka said.

Naruto opened his eyes to see Iruka beaming at him. But his sensei looked strange, like something was missing from his face...

Naruto's hand shot up to his forehead and felt the engraved insignia of the Ninja of the Leaves.

"Congratulations, graduate," Iruka said warmly. He felt shy all of a sudden, so he closed his eyes and kept talking.

"This calls for a celebration. Ichiraku Ramen, my treat," he said.

Iruka instantly felt two small arms wrap around him in a giant bear hug.

"Owww! I'm hurt, remember? Take it easy!" Iruka yelled. But he was still smiling.

"Sorry, sensei!" Naruto said merrily.

mansion, the Hokage looked up from his
ed.

kept   49   ttled at least. But the future still worries
self.

:hunin had hung around the mansion,

discussing how to flush Naruto out from his hideaway. The Hokage decided to send them home.

"But the decree should still stand," he muttered, heading for the door. "No one needs to know that Naruto has discovered the truth. That boy shouldn't suffer more than he already has."

He opened the door and was surprised to see a tall, thin man lurking in the shadows.

"Oh! You're early," the Hokage said.

"You have business for me, Lord Hokage?" the man asked as he stepped into the light.

He wore a mask over his nose and mouth, and his Leaf headband was slanted to cover his left eye. Beautiful silver hair stood up from his head in tufts.

"Your next novices have been chosen, Kakashi."

"So soon? But the graduation exam was just yesterday. This *is* unusual," Kakashi said in a slow drawl. His right eye drooped down at the corner, giving him a sleepy look.

"This case is special. But I should warn you, all three carry lots of baggage, and I am not referring to their backpacks," the Hokage went on.

"I'm ready for them. Think they'll be able to advance this time?" Kakashi asked.

The Hokage shrugged.

"Depends. Hopefully one or two will become village ninja at least. Please train them well."

Now it was Kakashi's turn to shrug.

"What will be will be. Especially if they are who you say they are."

The Hokage nodded and looked back at his crystal ball. Naruto was still holding fast to Iruka. The Hokage turned away and sighed.

SOMETHING ABOUT NARUTO

Later that week, the Hokage was smoking his pipe in front of the Great Stone Faces when Iruka walked by.

"Iruka! Just the person I wanted to see," the Hokage called out.

"Is there business to attend to, Lord Hokage?"

"Not really. I've just been wondering how Naruto is."

"He's definitely on a roll," Iruka chuckled. "I gave him a good talking-to, but he still keeps bragging about how he'll show everybody when he's a ninja." Iruka couldn't help smiling, but the Hokage looked grim.

"His dream may never come true," the Hokage said quietly.

"What do you mean?"

The Hokage took a puff on his pipe.

"You know, the Fourth Hokage wanted the villagers to see Naruto as a hero."

"Really?" Iruka said with surprise.

"And he is!" the Hokage insisted. "His tiny body was sacrificed for the village and the world beyond. What is he but a hero?"

Iruka nodded solemnly.

"But the villagers don't agree," the Hokage said sadly. "You can't really blame them. That beast took their village, their comrades, and their leader."

The Hokage frowned and lowered his voice.

"And their children are just like them. The decree has kept them from knowing just why Naruto's a pariah. But they follow their parents' example and reject him, too."

"I know, Lord Hokage," Iruka sighed.

"The sad fact is, if the villagers won't accept Naruto now, will they ever accept him as a ninja?" the Hokage asked.

Iruka thought hard for a moment.

"The villagers will be tough on Naruto," he admitted. "But I think he has the guts to overcome all that."

The Hokage gazed at the Great Stone Faces with a faraway look in his eyes.

"Naruto is still a child," he finally said. "Do you really think he can?"

Iruka didn't answer. The Hokage was right. Iruka had thought Naruto was just like himself, but there was one crucial difference between them.

The villagers don't hate me, Iruka thought. *They don't exactly love me, but they don't make faces behind my back.*

Naruto was more than just lonely. The way the adults looked down on him had hurt him to the very core.

"Naruto's had a rough time of it," Iruka said softly. "I never realized how rough until just recently."

"Ah, well. Don't worry too much, Iruka," the Hokage said kindly. "Naruto is still making strides despite everything. Why, just last week we thought he'd never graduate."

"That's true," Iruka had to admit.

"I'm handing Naruto over to Kakashi," the Hokage said bluntly. "He needs more attention than an ordinary jonin can give."

Iruka looked shocked.

"Kakashi? You mean, *that* Kakashi?"

"Yes, Kakashi Hatake. A jonin like him will be a good match for Naruto. Who knows if Naruto is even ninja material? But his powers could be extraordinary."

"Who are the other members of his squad?" Iruka asked with interest.

"One will be Sakura Haruno," the Hokage replied. "They say she's a real genius."

"She's very good at written tests," Iruka agreed. "She also has an excellent memory."

The Hokage nodded and continued.

"The other is Sasuke Uchiha."

"Uchiha? From the Uchiha Clan?" Iruka gasped.

"You know him, of course," the Hokage said.

"Of course," Iruka said. "Sasuke came in first this

term."

"The villagers think highly of him," the Hokage said, "though he does have some problems."

Iruka tried to remember what he knew about Sasuke. There was definitely something special about that boy...

"Oh! He's the last survivor of the Uchiha Clan! The rest of them died a few years ago, right?"

"Yes," the Hokage said quietly.

"Come to think of it, Sasuke is as much of a loner as Naruto," Iruka said thoughtfully. "The only difference is, Sasuke pushes people away from him."

The Hokage sadly shook his head.

"How can someone so young even be a loner? He has his reasons, I guess. In any case, he needs someone like Kakashi to keep him in line."

Sasuke's skills were still a bit crude, but he was already close to chunin level. There was no telling how good he might be in a few years.

"Eh, I've said enough already," the Hokage shrugged. "I wanted you to know about Naruto, but keep the rest under your headband, will you?"

Iruka bowed deeply. He'd been fretting about Naruto's future for days. Once Naruto went into training, Iruka would hardly see him, but at least he'd be in good hands.

And Iruka was grateful for that.

THREE'S A CROWD

"You're all qualified ninja now," Iruka boomed from the podium. "But remember, you're still only genin. From now on, your jonin leader will guide you and the rest of your squad."

Naruto barely heard what Iruka was saying. He was lost in his own dream world, a world where he was a brave ninja performing death-defying deeds.

While Naruto battled the beasts in his head, Iruka started to announce the three-member squads who would work together during the next stage of training.

"Squad Seven. Sakura Haruno, Naruto Uzumaki..." Iruka read from a long list.

"Sakura? What about Sakura?" Naruto blurted, popping awkwardly out of his seat. He quickly glanced around to see where she was.

Sakura sat two rows over, looking like she'd just lost her best friend. She was taller than Naruto, with pale pink hair that framed her face. Sometimes Naruto stared at Sakura when he thought she wasn't looking. But despite all his gawking, there was one thing about Sakura that Naruto had never noticed.

She hated him. Okay, she didn't exactly hate Naruto, but she did find him rather icky. To Sakura, Naruto was just a wild little monkey with wacko hair, not worth worrying about.

"And the third member of Squad Seven is Sasuke Uchiha," Iruka said.

"Woo hoo!" Sakura shouted, pumping her arms with excitement.

Naruto, on the other hand, was flabbergasted.

Sasuke peered up through his long black bangs. He was another problem child, but in a different way from Naruto. Though Sasuke's ninjutsu skills were top-notch, his people skills were way below par, a fatal flaw for a budding shinobi. He ignored his classmates, barely listened to his sensei, and could be a real stubborn so-and-so.

Sasuke glanced at Naruto and Sakura without interest, then quickly looked the other way.

"But I thought I'd be with Sakura! Not with this jerk!" Naruto whined.

"You took the words right out of my mouth, stupid," Sasuke snapped. "Just stay out of my way, okay?"

"Hey! You're the stupid one, you stupid stupid stupid-head!" Naruto sputtered, clenching his fists. He was getting all red in the face.

"I'm warning you, Naruto! Keep away from Sasuke or else!" a voice snarled behind him.

Naruto nervously swung around. Sakura stood with her hands on her hips, glaring at him like a fiend.

"But, Sakura! This guy is really—"

"Shut up, Naruto!" Sakura snarled. "Go sit somewhere else, okay?"

Naruto shuffled to the other side of the room, while Sakura sat down near Sasuke. Iruka tried hard not to smile.

So long for now, Naruto, he thought wistfully as he continued reading from his list.

Naruto plopped down and glared at the floor, his cheeks still blazing.

"Uh, hi, Naruto. Too bad we can't be in the same squad," a girl stammered from nearby. Naruto looked up.

Hinata Hyuga was right in front of him, twirling a lock of her dark blue hair.

"Yeah," Naruto muttered.

Hinata blushed and looked away, but she kept on talking in her soft, shy voice.

"M-maybe the jonin will change the squads later," she suggested hopefully. "Then we can be together for sure."

"Whatever," Naruto sighed. He put his head down on the table and pretended to go to sleep.

Hinata watched Naruto for a long, sad moment.

"Well, see you," she finally said, and crept back to her seat.

"Sheesh! I always attract the weirdoes," Naruto muttered under his breath.

He was still too young to care about Hinata's feelings, or to realize she even had them. There would come a time when Naruto would hate himself for being such a colossal jerk. But not today.

Naruto soon dozed off for real. He slept for what seemed like hours until Sakura's angry voice woke him up.

"Well! Guess they forgot about us," she was muttering.

Naruto looked up groggily. They were the only people left in the classroom.

"Wh-what's goin' on?" he mumbled.

"The other squads left a long time ago," Sakura said. "Our guy hasn't even shown up."

"That stinks!" Naruto griped. He eyed Sasuke, who was sitting by himself, quietly fuming.

What a slimebag, Naruto thought. *What does Sakura see in that creep?*

Naruto felt restless all of a sudden, so he tore through the classroom to find something to do. He spotted a dusty chalkboard eraser and got an evil gleam in his eye.

"Hey! What are you doing?" Sakura demanded to know.

"Just punishing a tardy teacher," Naruto said lightly.

He wedged the eraser at the top of the sliding door and skipped back to his seat.

"Well, I'm not bailing you out when you get busted," she sniveled, but she didn't move the eraser.

"You guys are so incredibly dumb," Sasuke sniffed. "He'd never fall for a trick like that."

The door suddenly clacked open. The eraser bounced off the silver head of a tall, thin jonin. *Their* jonin.

"See, Sasuke? He fell for it!" Naruto hissed.

"Sorry, sensei!" Sakura said in a rush. "I tried to stop him, honest!"

He didn't answer. His droopy right eye gave him a dreamy look.

Why does he wear his headband like that? Naruto thought. *Is he trying to hide a scar?*

He has a mask over his mouth, Sakura noticed. *Is something wrong with his teeth?*

Is this guy really a jonin? Sasuke wondered.

Their new leader stared at them for a while. Then he spoke in a dull voice, as though he'd rather be anywhere but there.

"Well. You wanna know what I think of you three?"

The brand-new ninja looked nervous, but the jonin cut right to the chase.

"I don't like your kind," he drawled.

"But why?" Sakura gasped. Naruto looked stunned, and even stone-faced Sasuke was frowning.

"Relax, little girl," the jonin assured her. "It won't affect your final grade."

"What do you mean?" Sakura begged.

"You'll find out later—even if you don't want to," he said ominously. But behind his mask he smiled.

THE FIRST TEST

Squad Seven went to the training ground early the next morning, just as Kakashi had told them to do. But two hours later, he was still a no-show.

"I can't believe he's late again," Sakura huffed. They griped and moaned to each other until a jolly voice greeted them from behind.

"Morning, everybody!" Kakashi sang out.

"You're laaaate!" Naruto and Sakura whined in unison. Sasuke just glared. Out of all the jonin in the world, why did they have to wind up with this one?

Kakashi ignored them and reached into a pouch at his waist. He took out two small bells on strings and started swinging them around. They tinkled lightly in the breeze.

"See these bells?" he said. "Today's test is to grab 'em from me by lunchtime."

Nobody answered. Squad Seven was still outraged at being kept waiting again.

Kakashi walked over to three large logs that were planted in the ground, and put a clock atop the middle log.

"This alarm goes off at high noon. If you don't have a bell, you don't get lunch," he explained. "However, you can watch me eat mine."

Three hungry stomachs growled in harmony.

"But you told us not to eat breakfast today!" Sakura complained.

"Yup, I sure did," Kakashi nodded.

Nobody said anything, but each member of Squad Seven was thinking along similar lines.

That jerk tricked us!

That jerk said breakfast would make us throw up!

That jerk is a dirty liar!

While Squad Seven silently fumed, Kakashi smoothly continued.

"Now you're probably wondering why there are only two bells," he said.

He jangled them again. It was really getting irritating.

"It's simple," Kakashi said. "If you don't get a bell, you go right back to the academy."

"What?" Naruto and Sakura gasped. Sasuke's mouth fell open, but he didn't say a word.

Kakashi slapped his forehead in dismay.

"Oh, gee! Did I forget to tell you?" he said innocently. "This test is also to see if you can make it as a genin."

"But we never heard about that," Sakura complained.

"Wh-what do you mean?" Naruto sputtered.

Sasuke just glared, but Kakashi kept his cool.

"C'mon, crew. Did you really think that doing the Clone Jutsu automatically makes you a ninja?"

Squad Seven looked thoughtful. They definitely had a lot to learn.

"So if we pass this test, will we really be ninja?" Sakura asked hopefully.

"Hmm, I suppose so," Kakashi said vaguely, ringing the bells again.

Sasuke got right in his face. "You're keeping something from us," he accused.

Kakashi quickly looked away.

"Some things are better left unsaid. If you knew everything, you'd wimp out for sure."

"No fair that you know, but we don't," Sasuke griped.

Kakashi raised his right eyebrow.

"So that's how you talk to a sensei, eh? Interesting."

Sasuke fell silent but his angry face kept on talking. Kakashi paused for effect, then continued.

"By the way, only one out of three people pass," he said. "We have twenty-seven genin this year, so only nine will make the cut."

"Wh-what happens to the rest?" Naruto stammered.

"Like I said before, they go back to the academy. They'll keep on training until they can pass the test."

"Noooooo!" Sakura cried.

"Who cares. *I'm* gonna pass," Sasuke grumbled.

"My! Such confidence," Kakashi said. "Wonder where you get it from."

"I don't have time to fool around," Sasuke muttered.

"I see."

Kakashi put his hands on his hips and looked at each of them in turn.

"So that's the way it is," he said bluntly. "If you wanna pass, use everything you've got. Fists, feet, razor-sharp weapons..."

"But that sounds dangerous, sensei!" Sakura said with horror.

"You didn't even see that eraser!" Naruto chimed in. "We could kill you! Or maim you! Or, or..."

Kakashi sighed as Naruto babbled on.

"Sheesh! Such big talk for a little guy! Dead last in his class, yet he still thinks he's a Hokage."

"D-dead last?" Naruto gulped.

"I saw your grades, m'boy! Your sensei really took pity on you."

Naruto blushed. Kakashi turned away from him.

"Okay, everybody," he said. "When I say 'go'..."

Naruto didn't wait to hear the rest. He grabbed a shuriken from his holster and prepared to attack.

A strong hand instantly grabbed Naruto's arm from behind, while another tugged his hair.

"Relax, Naruto," Kakashi drawled. "I didn't say 'go' yet."

"How'd he do that?" Sasuke muttered.

"Boy, is he fast," Sakura said with awe.

Naruto blinked in surprise. Just a second ago, Kakashi was standing at least ten feet in front of him. Weird thing was, Naruto never even saw him move.

"So, Naruto! Think I can take care of myself now?" Kakashi teased.

Naruto couldn't help smiling. Maybe this guy wasn't so bad after all!

"Okay, then!" Kakashi yelled. "On your mark! Get set!"

The members of Squad Seven held their breaths.

"Go!!!"

The three fanned out in different directions. While his students disappeared, Kakashi casually ambled to the center of the field.

"Good," he said, nodding with approval. "At least you two know the basics."

He was referring to Sasuke and Sakura. As soon as Kakashi had given the signal, both had suppressed their presences and hidden from sight, a skill that suited almost any situation.

Naruto's approach, however, was a bit different.

"Okay, you! Gimme that bell!" he screeched, clenching his fists.

"Your technique *is* unusual," Kakashi said mildly.

"Oh, yeah? So's your haircut!" Naruto sneered. He

charged toward Kakashi at full speed.

"Shinobi Battle Skill Number One: taijutsu," Kakashi said calmly.

"You mean hand-to-hand combat?" Naruto puffed. He was really running hard.

Kakashi watched Naruto out of the corner of his eye and dug around in his pouch again. Suddenly Naruto slammed on the brakes.

Uh-oh! Sensei has a weapon! he thought with alarm.

But Kakashi didn't pull out a shuriken, or a kunai, or even a soggy spitball. He pulled out a paperback book. Naruto squinted to read the title. It was called *Make-Out Paradise.*

"Wh-what's that?" Naruto asked.

"What? Never seen a book before?" Kakashi scoffed.

"But why do you have one?"

"I have lots of free time. Besides, I'm dying to see what happens next in this thing."

"Free time?" Naruto said, looking surprised.

"Don't worry, Naruto. I can train you and read at the same time," Kakashi assured him. He dove right into the story and was soon lost to the world.

Naruto cooled his heels for a while, but soon grew impatient.

"He's asking for it!" Naruto muttered, blood rushing to his head. He clenched his right fist and zoomed toward Kakashi, who didn't look up from his book.

And so the battle began! Naruto wildly swung his fist! Kakashi blocked the punch and kept on reading. Naruto wildly swung his foot! Kakashi ducked the kick and kept on reading. Then Naruto got off balance and spun off to the side, his back toward Kakashi.

"Shoot!" Naruto groaned as he tried to turn around. Suddenly he heard Kakashi's voice right behind him.

"You fool. A ninja never shows his back twice," Kakashi said calmly. He leaned forward and stuck out the first two fingers of each hand.

"Leaf Village Secret Finger Jutsu: A Thousand Years of Death!!!" he yelled, aiming his fingers at Naruto's butt.

Naruto screamed as he flew up into the air. He sailed across the field and splashed into the nearby river. As Naruto sank to the bottom, he threw shuriken wildly in Kakashi's direction.

Miraculously, they spun right to their intended target. Kakashi stuck out his index finger and caught every shuriken by its center hole...and kept on reading.

"Nooooo!" Naruto howled, swallowing a mouthful of muddy water. Suddenly he saw the eyes of people from his life spinning around his head in a kaleidoscope.

He saw the hateful eyes of Mizuki. The cold eyes of the villagers. And then another, kinder pair of eyes. The warm eyes of Iruka.

Naruto is actually an excellent student.

I can't stop now! Naruto vowed to himself. If something

happened to him, Iruka would be devastated.

Naruto made a sign and concentrated with all his might. *I'll get that bell no matter what!*

Kakashi was still deep into *Make-Out Paradise* when Naruto crawled out onto the riverbank, coughing and spitting.

"Don't forget. No bell, no lunch," Kakashi said mildly as he turned a page.

Naruto's stomach started growling again.

"I know that already!" he snapped.

Kakashi snickered and kept on reading. Suddenly Naruto got a bright idea. He was so hungry he could barely move, but now he knew what he had to do.

No matter what.

Kakashi sensed some movement behind him and swung around to look. Naruto clones were leaping out of the river like big angry goldfish.

"I will become a ninja!" they cried in unison.

They landed around Kakashi, completely encircling him. He looked around with interest, but didn't seem the least bit shocked.

"A forbidden jutsu from the Scroll of Sealing, eh?" he chuckled. "Nice. Bet you can't keep it going for long."

Naruto grinned. Suddenly Kakashi looked surprised as a soaking-wet Naruto pounced on his back.

"Shame on you, Kakashi-sensei!" the Naruto sneered. "You said a ninja should never show his back!"

Kakashi turned to look at the Naruto behind him, completely missing the Naruto who jumped in front of him.

That Naruto socked Kakashi right in the face. But right before the fist made contact, Kakashi became a Naruto, too!

"No fair! You used the Transformation Jutsu!" the Narutos yelled.

They suddenly panicked and started pummeling each other. From a nearby treetop, someone was watching the whole mad scene with derision.

"That's not the Transformation Jutsu. That's the Replacement Jutsu, stupid," Sasuke muttered.

The Replacement Jutsu is a not a top-level skill, but very effective when used correctly. A ninja quickly replaces his body with something else, human or otherwise, to fool his opponent and cause total chaos.

Needless to say, Naruto was the perfect victim.

Naruto finally realized that making shadow clones was getting him nowhere. He shut them all down and stood by himself, desperately wondering what to do next.

All of a sudden, Naruto spotted something small and shiny on the root of a nearby tree. Hold on! Could it be? He buzzed toward it like a mad hornet.

There it was, plain as day. One of Kakashi's bells!

"Well, well! What have we here?" Naruto chortled. "Looks like I get lunch after all."

Naruto happily reached for the golden prize. Two seconds later, he was hanging from a branch by his feet!

"You moron! Couldn't you see it was a trap?" Sasuke hissed at Naruto, who was swinging back and forth like a wind chime.

"You're too trusting, Naruto," Kakashi said.

He calmly stooped down to pick up the bell before he gave Naruto a cold hard look.

"A ninja always reads between the lines. Got it?"

"I know all that!" Naruto whimpered.

"I don't really think you do," Kakashi coolly replied.

Suddenly, Sasuke saw the perfect opportunity. He darted behind a tree and started tossing shuriken with lightning speed. They looked like they were coming from completely different directions, but every one of them hit Kakashi.

Or did they?

"What the—?" Sasuke gasped.

He rushed over to where Kakashi had been standing. In his place was a large log stuck with shuriken.

He had fallen for one of Kakashi's traps! Granted, it was way more complicated than the trap that felled Naruto, but Sasuke couldn't believe he didn't see it coming.

He lured me on purpose, Sasuke suddenly realized. *Now he knows where I am.* He took off without looking back.

Sakura, who'd been hiding nearby, took her cue from Sasuke and crept away. She was never that great at physical stuff, but she had a real talent for grasping situations.

She quickly figured out that Kakashi had baited Sasuke. But no matter how hard she tried to sense Sasuke's presence, she still couldn't find him. Poor Sakura got so obsessed, she never realized that she was about to become Kakashi's third victim.

Sakura was still looking for Sasuke when she saw Kakashi leaning against a tree, reading his book. She ducked behind another tree and held her breath, but Kakashi didn't go away.

It's okay. He didn't see me, she told herself.

"Sakura! Behind you!" someone shouted.

Sakura swung around to see Kakashi gaping at her with one big scary eyeball. She opened her mouth, but nothing came out.

There was no wind, but suddenly the leaves on the ground rose up and spun around her like a hurricane. Sakura stood in the eye of storm with a blank look on her face.

Then the leaves fell to earth again. Sakura looked around for Kakashi.

No one was there.

She started creeping back through the forest. All of a sudden, someone desperately called her name.

"Sakura! Sakura!"

She stopped dead in her tracks.

"Sasuke?" she shrieked.

She dashed in the direction of his voice and soon found him, sprawled over the root of a big tree. Shuriken were stuck in his arms, his legs, everywhere.

"S-Sakura. H-help me," Sasuke choked, gasping for breath.

Sakura's piercing scream echoed through the forest. She started sweating and crying and foaming at the mouth, all at the same time. It was not a pretty sight.

"Uh-oh. Guess I overdid it a little," Kakashi murmured.

Meanwhile, the real Sasuke heard Sakura scream and carefully looked around. A lazy voice spoke up behind him.

"Shinobi Battle Skill Number Two: genjutsu, the art of illusion. Sakura was an easy target, but maybe I was too harsh."

Sasuke turned to see Kakashi leaning against another tree, reading *Make-Out Paradise.*

"I'm different from the other two," Sasuke muttered.

Kakashi glanced up from his book.

"Save that line until you have a bell," he grunted. "I'm looking forward to fighting the last of the Uchiha Clan."

Sasuke didn't bother to answer as he dashed away.

Soon shuriken flew even faster at Kakashi. He expertly dodged them all, though each one still came from a different direction.

"How do I get it through your thick skull, Sasuke?"

Kakashi sighed. "Attacking is not the answer here."

Sasuke grinned from his hiding place and threw another shuriken. Now Kakashi looked surprised. The path of this shuriken was very unlike the others.

It's a trap! Kakashi realized.

The shuriken sliced open a holding net, sending scores of sharp daggers sailing toward Kakashi. Luckily, Kakashi had predicted this would happen, and swerved off to the side in the nick of time.

But Sasuke had figured Kakashi would do that, so he was there ready and waiting for him.

He came up behind Kakashi and slammed a kick in his direction. Kakashi grabbed Sasuke's hand and foot and flipped him upside down. But Sasuke had figured he'd do that, too, and quickly aimed a punch at Kakashi's jaw. Kakashi blocked the blow with his elbow.

Sasuke was getting desperate. All of his attacks had been foiled, and now Kakashi was dangling him like a cat.

But Sasuke didn't give in. Keeping Kakashi's arms occupied was actually his master plan.

Sasuke stretched to grab the bell that was just out of his reach. But Kakashi was onto him like flies on dog poo.

He dropped Sasuke and jumped backwards, out of reach. Kakashi grimaced as sweat dribbled down his forehead.

"Do you ever give up? I wanna get back to my book," he grumbled.

Sasuke paused to catch his breath. He was huffing and puffing like crazy, but still not ready to surrender.

"Well. Maybe you are different from the other guys," Kakashi had to admit.

But he calmly faced Sasuke again. One thing was dead certain: no matter how ferociously Sasuke attacked him, Kakashi would never lose his cool.

The clock was ticking away. For Sasuke, this wasn't just about lunch. His very pride was at stake here.

He stood up straight as a chopstick and quickly made a complex sign.

"Tiger! Horse!" Sasuke yelled, arching his back. "Fire Style: Fireball Jutsu!!!"

He can't do that! Kakashi thought with shock. *He doesn't have enough chakra!*

Red-hot flames roared out of Sasuke's mouth. They scorched a wide section of earth, then quickly disappeared.

So did Kakashi.

Where'd he go? thought Sasuke with alarm. Did the jutsu get rid of him? Or did he escape?

Sasuke looked around in a frenzy. Suddenly a strong hand grabbed his ankle and squeezed.

"Guess what, Sasuke? I'm under you!" Kakashi snickered.

"Noooooo!"

"Earth Style: Headhunter Jutsu," Kakashi drawled.

Sasuke was too exhausted to resist. His body was instantly pulled underground, leaving just his head exposed.

"So! How's it feel to be buried alive?" Kakashi joked.

Sasuke glared at him. Kakashi snorted with amusement.

"Shinobi Battle Skill Number Three: ninjutsu, the art of stealth. But you were right, Sasuke. You are different from the other two."

Sasuke glared at him again.

"You know what they say," Kakashi shrugged as he walked away. "The nail that sticks up gets hammered down."

Sasuke kept on glaring.

Meanwhile, Naruto was still hanging from the tree by his feet. Even though he was upside down, he saw two bento boxes and two sets of chopsticks atop a square stone monument nearby.

Naruto pulled out his kunai and wriggled and squirmed until he finally cut the rope around his ankles. He fell to the ground with a plop, scrambled to his feet, and headed for the food.

He tiptoed around the stone, looking for traps. Everything seemed okay, so he grabbed a box and sat down.

"Who cares if I don't get a bell?" Naruto sniggered. "I still get lunch!"

He split apart some chopsticks and plucked up a juicy morsel of fish. But before he could pop it into his mouth, Naruto suddenly felt a very familiar presence.

"Hello, Naruto," Kakashi said.

"Th-this is a joke, sensei! Honest!" Naruto sputtered.

"Too late, you fool."

Just then the alarm rang.

FOOD FOR THOUGHT

Back at the training ground, Squad Seven had been waiting for what seemed like hours. Naruto was tied firmly to the center log, while Sakura and Sasuke stood mutely on either side of him.

All three were weak with hunger and mad as heck at Kakashi. No doubt about it, they were not happy little genin.

"I can still hear your stomachs," Kakashi said.

He folded his arms across his chest and fixed his right eye on each one in turn. Finally he spoke.

"Here's the deal, crew. Nobody goes back to the academy."

Naruto stopped squirming and suddenly looked elated.

"What? You mean we all passed?" he shrieked.

Kakashi's right eye twinkled for a second. Then he broke the bad news.

"Nope! You all flunked."

Squad Seven looked stunned.

"What do you mean?" Naruto yelped.

Kakashi's right eye lost its merry twinkle.

"Not one of you brats has any business being a ninja," he said coldly.

Sasuke broke ranks and charged at the sensei like a wild boar.

"Sasuke!" Sakura gasped.

Kakashi effortlessly brought Sasuke down. Then he sat on Sasuke's back and planted a foot on his head.

"See? That's why you're a brat," Kakashi snapped.

Sasuke's face turned as red as an umeboshi plum. Kakashi glared at Naruto and Sakura.

"Why do you think we assigned you to squads? Huh?"

Squad Seven looked flustered.

"You really don't know the answer, do you?" Kakashi persisted.

"Wh-what answer?" stammered Naruto.

"The answer that tells me whether you pass this test or not."

"But how should we know? You never told us!" Sakura protested.

Kakashi shook his head in disbelief.

"C'mon! What's the answer?" begged Naruto.

"It's teamwork," Kakashi barked.

Squad Seven looked uncomfortable.

"If you three had attacked me together, you might have stood a fighting chance."

Sakura suddenly looked defiant.

"Then why were there only two bells?" she asked pointedly. "Even if we did take them, someone would still miss lunch. You call that teamwork?"

"Sure."

Kakashi cleared his throat and continued.

"This test was meant to put you at odds with each other," he explained. "I wanted to see if you'd join forces. But instead..."

Kakashi stopped talking and shook his head. Then he sadly looked at Sakura.

"You didn't even try to help Naruto. All you cared about was Sasuke."

Sakura swallowed hard and stared down at her feet.

"Naruto tried to do the work of three ninja," Kakashi continued. "And Sasuke decided he was better off alone, without you two lamebrains."

Sasuke's face turned even redder.

"Remember, you're a team! Your ninjutsu skills matter, but working together is even more important."

Kakashi suddenly pulled a kunai from his pouch and held it against Sasuke's neck.

"Going solo can put your comrades in grave danger," he said calmly.

"Wh-what are you going to do?" Sakura gasped.

"Sakura! Kill Naruto—or I'll kill Sasuke!"

"What?"

"Hurry up, girl! Don't you care if Sasuke croaks?"

Sakura frantically looked back and forth between Sasuke and Naruto. For a few tense moments, nobody said a word. Then Kakashi shrugged and let Sasuke go.

"Something like this could really happen," Kakashi said grimly. "A ninja's life is always on the line."

He pointed at the monument.

"See the names carved on that stone? Every ninja there was a village hero."

"Did you say hero? All right!" Naruto yelled out. "Someday my name will be on there, too!"

Kakashi gave him a piercing look.

"Those ninja were more than heroes. They all died in the line of duty," he said, his voice wavering. "Some of them were my best friends..."

He patted the top of the stone with affection, then turned back to Squad Seven looking stern.

"You guys get one last chance," he said flatly. "But I'm warning you, this afternoon will be even tougher. And whatever you do, don't feed Naruto."

"Why not?" Naruto whined.

"You broke the rules, remember? Whoever gives Naruto food will be out on their ear."

"But, sensei—" Sakura started to say.

"I call the shots here. Understand?"

Kakashi took off with his book for parts unknown. The three stood for a while in a stupor.

Finally Sasuke reached for a bento box. Sakura followed his lead and took the other one.

Naruto's stomach growled in protest, but he shut his eyes and looked the other way.

Sasuke and Sakura chewed as quietly as they could. All of a sudden, Sasuke stopped eating. He heaved a big sigh and took the rest of his lunch to Naruto.

"What's this?" Naruto asked with surprise.

"No, Sasuke!" Sakura warned. "Sensei said not to share!"

Sasuke gave her a sharp look.

"We have to take those bells together," he said firmly. "Naruto can't help if he's starving to death."

Sakura looked longingly at the rest of her lunch, but she also shared her leftovers. Naruto was about to thank her when smoke suddenly surrounded them.

"What's going on here?" Kakashi hollered, bursting through the dark cloud.

Sakura screamed and turned white as tofu. Naruto squirmed wildly on the log, trying to get loose. Sasuke kept quiet, but sweat dripped down his face.

Kakashi stared at Squad Seven with his good right eye. Then he gave them the thumbs up sign.

"Everybody passes!" he shouted with glee.

Squad Seven looked stunned.

"It's not my fault, sensei! I never once begged for rice!" Naruto swore.

"Didn't you hear me? You all passed the test!"

"But we ignored your orders," Sasuke said.

"Big deal," Kakashi scoffed. "Any blockhead can follow orders. I wanted you three to cooperate—and you finally did!"

"But, sensei! Does that mean—" Naruto started to say.

Kakashi suddenly looked wistful.

"Ninja who break rules are scum," he said softly. "But ninja who don't help their comrades are even worse."

Naruto's heart was almost bursting out of his chest. The verdict was in. In Naruto's eyes, Kakashi was now the coolest shinobi ever.

"School's over, crew," Kakashi said. "Tomorrow, we go on assignment."

The members of Squad Seven were genin at last. But their toughest lessons still lay ahead of them.

SQUAD SEVEN TAKES A JOB

On the continent where Naruto lived were Five Great Nations: the Land of Water, the Land of Lightning, the Land of Wind, the Land of Earth, and the Land of Fire. Each Great Nation had a self-ruled shinobi village in charge of that nation's military.

Each shinobi village was led by a ninja of the elite kage rank. These Five Kage were the best shinobi of all. They were the Mizukage of Hidden Mist, the Raikage of Hidden Cloud, the Kazekage of Hidden Sand, the Tsuchikage of Hidden Stone, and last but not least, the Hokage of Hidden Leaf, Naruto's village in the Land of Fire.

"Hey! Why doesn't the Land of Waves have a shinobi village?" Naruto asked.

It was a bright spring day. Kakashi and Squad Seven were headed for the Land of Waves on their very first assignment, guarding an old bridge builder named Tazuna.

"The Land of Waves is surrounded by the sea," Kakashi explained. "It doesn't need as much protection as countries that share borders."

"That's why I hired you beginners," Tazuna said.

He was in excellent shape for his advanced age, from years of hard physical labor. He wore small wire-rimmed eyeglasses and a cone-shaped hat with a pointy tip. His breath smelled faintly of booze.

"Who's trying to hunt you down?" Naruto babbled. "Is building a bridge dangerous?"

Tazuna rolled his eyes. Naruto's constant chatter was getting on his nerves.

"Our location is very hazardous. It's, uh, hard to concentrate on our work."

Kakashi could tell Tazuna was losing patience, so he tried to spare him from more of Naruto's irritating questions.

"C'mon, Naruto! What were you expecting from a C-rank assignment? War?" Kakashi kidded.

Village ninja assignments were ranked from A (the toughest) to D (the easiest). While D-rank jobs included baby-sitting and looking for lost pets, C-rank assignments could be a little more challenging, such as guarding people who lived in safer areas.

People who hired ninja paid on a sliding scale, depending on what rank the assignment rated. But they only had to pay if the job went as planned.

Shinobi villages always needed money, though their nations did help them financially. So for the good of the village, a ninja accepted any assignment, no matter how boring it might be.

Naruto had his hopes, however.

"Maybe the robbers who attack him will be ninja!" he said breathlessly. "If I bash in their heads, Grandpa Hokage will give us a better job next time!"

"Don't be stupid," Kakashi said. He playfully knocked on Naruto's head to check for brains.

Sakura threw Naruto an icy glare.

"You're so dumb! We could die if we face real ninja before we're ready! Right, Sasuke?"

Sasuke didn't answer.

"Easy, everybody!" Kakashi joked. "This is just your first assignment. You don't have to push so hard."

He turned to Tazuna, who was walking beside him.

"We won't have to worry about ninja, right? Just plain old robbers and thugs?"

"Uh, r-right," Tazuna said, quickly looking the other way.

They came to a big puddle in the middle of the road. Everybody stepped around it and kept on walking.

Their journey was off to a great start. The weather was fine, a soft breeze was blowing, and the birds were chirping in the trees.

Naruto happily flung out his arms and gazed up at the

clear blue sky.

"Ahhhh! What a perfect day to begin my quest to become the Hokage!"

"Do you ever shut up?" Sakura snapped.

Sasuke, as usual, was in a world all his own. Then suddenly his mouth twitched. He swung around to look at Kakashi, who brought up the rear of their little group.

"Sensei!" Sasuke cried out.

It was too late.

Two figures slowly rose up from the big puddle behind them. Their outfits looked strange, but they were obviously ninja. They wore masks over their mouths, headbands with devil horns, and gloves tipped with sharp metal claws. Each ninja also sported a cylinder around his wrist, like a big clunky bracelet.

Quick as a flash, metal chains flew out of the cylinders with a loud clang. The ninja wrapped them round and round Kakashi with blinding speed. The chains were studded with sharp teeth that dug into Kakashi's flesh.

"One down," a ninja hissed.

They pulled the chains even tighter. Kakashi's body began to crumble.

"Sensei!" screamed Sakura.

Naruto stood frozen with shock, gaping at the gruesome scene.

"Two down," someone hissed right behind him.

I'm gonna die! Naruto thought wildly. He knew he

should try to escape, but he couldn't move one muscle.

More chains were spit from the cylinders. The ninja cracked them like whips. Naruto stood between them, rooted to the spot. He looked back with terror as the chains moved closer and closer.

Suddenly, a shuriken hit the chains and pinned them to a tree trunk. Sasuke dashed up and stabbed his kunai through the shuriken hole.

"Run away, you idiot!" he shouted at Naruto.

"C'mon, you blasted chains!" the ninja roared, trying to yank them down. But Sasuke had done his job well. The chains stayed put.

As the two ninja struggled, Sasuke saw his big chance. He ran up and kicked in both of the cylinders. Then he kicked both of the ninja in the head!

The ninja staggered backward for a moment, but they quickly recovered. They twisted the cylinders off their arms and chucked them to the ground. Then one went for Naruto, and the other went for Tazuna.

Naruto twisted to dodge the attack, but he was a second too late. The sharp metal claws grazed the back of his left hand.

"Yowwww!" Naruto wailed. He looked back at his enemy, but no one was there. Then he heard Sakura's voice.

"Mr. Tazuna! Run away!" she was screaming.

Naruto spun around in her direction.

Sakura stood between Tazuna and his attacker, holding her kunai at the ready. But she was looking around helplessly, like she didn't know what to do next.

Sasuke saw her plight and ran over to help. He jumped in front of Sakura and Tazuna and flung out both arms protectively. The ninja lunged closer to them, his claws poised to tear flesh.

Suddenly a strong arm shot out from behind and grabbed him in a chokehold. The ninja started to gag.

"Sensei!" Sakura shouted with joy.

Kakashi had already finished off the other ninja and was lugging him under his arm.

Naruto looked down at the pieces of Kakashi's flesh and saw broken chunks of wood.

"Kakashi-sensei!" he shouted. "You used the Replacement Jutsu!"

"Sorry I didn't help you sooner, Naruto," Kakashi said with feeling. "Are you hurt?"

Naruto looked at his left hand. The bright red gashes were turning ominously darker.

"I never dreamed you'd freeze up out there," Kakashi went on. "In any case, good job, Sasuke. You too, Sakura."

Naruto instantly felt the ground sink beneath him.

What a little wimp he was. He'd been ready to take on the world, but when push came to shove, he'd completely wussed out.

Naruto was being way too hard on himself. Most ninja-in-training screwed up on a regular basis. But Sasuke had saved his life—which made Naruto feel lower than pond scum.

Sasuke noticed Naruto staring at him.

"Are you hurt, chicken?" he sneered.

Naruto opened his mouth to yell back.

"Settle this later, Naruto," Kakashi said seriously. "Those claws were dipped in poison. You need to flush that stuff out of your bloodstream."

"B-but how?" Naruto shuddered.

"Open the wound wider so it will bleed. But keep still or the poison will spread inside your body."

Naruto looked at his hand again. It was starting to swell like a blowfish.

"We need to talk, Tazuna," said Kakashi gravely.

"R-really? About what?"

Kakashi didn't answer. He tied the two knocked-out ninja to a tree, then carefully examined their equipment.

"These guys must be from the Hidden Mist Village," he concluded. "They keep on fighting no matter what."

Just then a ninja blinked his eyes open and looked straight at Kakashi.

"Can I ask you something?" he grumbled.

"Sure."

"How did you sense our first attack? It had to be completely unexpected."

"Not really," Kakashi shrugged. "There's been no rain in these parts for days. That big puddle looked out of place."

The ninja quickly looked down in embarrassment.

Tazuna frowned at Kakashi.

"If you knew that, why did you let the kids face those fiends?"

"So I could watch them and figure out why they were here," Kakashi replied.

Tazuna swallowed hard.

"I could have killed them on the spot," Kakashi went on. "But then I'd never know who they were really after. Now I know for sure."

"Wh-what do you mean?" Tazuna stammered.

"Those guys wanted you, Tazuna. If we were their prey, they would have attacked us first and killed you later."

Tazuna stared at the ground as Kakashi continued.

"Are ninja after you? If so, that makes this a B-rank assignment at least. Did you lie when you hired us on?"

Tazuna didn't look up. Kakashi sighed.

"You probably had a good reason, but lying is strictly taboo. You broke our contract. This job is over."

"We're too young for an assignment like this," Sakura pointed out. "Besides, Naruto's hurt. We have to take him back to the village."

"She may be right," said Kakashi thoughtfully.

He glanced at Naruto, who was sweating profusely.

"Okay, then! Let's head home so Naruto can get his hand fixed."

Naruto felt ready to explode with frustration. This was all his fault! Their very first assignment would be scrubbed because of his stupid little injury.

Naruto gritted his teeth, whipped out his kunai, and plunged it into his left hand.

As everybody watched with shock, Naruto ripped the kunai through his flesh. Blood gushed out and dripped to the ground.

Why am I always so different? he thought with despair. *Why can't I ever fit in?*

"Naruto! What the heck are you doing?" Sakura gasped.

Naruto didn't answer, but he immediately made three promises to himself.

I will never be rescued again. I will never wuss out again. And I will never, ever let Sasuke show me up like that. I swear all this by the pain of my left hand.

Then he took a deep breath and confidently turned to the others.

"Naruto Uzumaki reporting for duty! I'm ready to protect Tazuna!"

SOME GUY NAMED GATO

In the middle of a lush forest sat a cabin shaped like a pine tree. The cabin blended in so nicely with the rest of the landscape, you could barely tell it was there. It was the perfect secret hideout.

Inside, a man in a black suit was having a hissy fit.

"I paid you guys a fortune! You said you were trained ex-ninja!" he screeched. He was short, ugly, and middle-aged, with round glasses that gave him an owlish look.

As the man raged on, a tall guy sat with his legs propped up, surrounded by ninja-in-waiting. He had thick black hair but no eyebrows, which gave his face a strange, unfinished look.

He wore a white mask over his mouth and his headband turned sideways, with the shield above one ear. He had on arm warmers but no shirt, showing off a lean chest rippled with muscles.

But his most eye-catching accessory was his sword.

The blade was as tall as a man and as wide as a butcher's cleaver. He swung the sword playfully at the man in black, like it was a little paring knife.

"Shut up, Gato. I've heard enough of your griping," he muttered. "I'll kill him myself with the Guillotine Sword."

He thrust the tip of the blade under the short man's nose. Gato's complexion was naturally pallid, but now he looked like a ghost. He broke out into a cold sweat and started to tremble, then spoke in a strangled voice.

"I...I just hope you succeed this time. Tazuna has hired some good ninja. They've already struck down the Demon Brothers."

"Don't you remember who I am?" the tall guy sneered. "I'm Zabuza Momochi, the Demon of the Hidden Mist."

Zabuza glared at Gato for a minute. Then he threw back his head and laughed.

Kakashi glanced at Naruto's left hand, which was still bleeding profusely.

"Watch out, Naruto!" he said breezily. "It's good to get out the poison, but if you bleed too much you'll die."

Kakashi sounded so nonchalant that Naruto didn't get what he meant at first. Then suddenly it dawned on him.

"No way! No way! I can't die like this!" Naruto yelled. He started pacing around frantically, leaving a trail of blood in his wake.

"Calm down, Naruto. Let me see."

Kakashi picked up Naruto's left hand and got a weird look on his face. The angry red gashes now looked like harmless little boo-boos. What was going on?

As Kakashi dabbed the hand with clean gauze, he saw another bizarre sight. The cuts seemed to be healing before his very eyes.

"Am I gonna be okay?" Naruto asked nervously. He figured his days were numbered since Kakashi looked so serious.

"Uh, sure! You'll be just fine, Naruto."

This is the power of the Nine-Tailed Fox, Kakashi thought as he bandaged Naruto's hand.

Inside this small boy's body, a boundless power flowed. Someday Naruto would have to learn how to harness this incredible force. If he didn't, his path would lead only to destruction.

"Kakashi-sensei? I want to tell you everything. Will you listen to me?"

Kakashi turned to face Tazuna, who looked contrite.

"The men after me aren't common thugs," Tazuna began.

"Tsk! I figured as much," Kakashi snorted.

Tazuna pointed to the ninja of the Hidden Mist.

"Ever hear the name Gato? They work for him," he said.

Kakashi looked surprised.

"You mean Gato as in the Gato Corporation? That guy

has made billions in shipping."

"His company is actually a front for smuggling drugs and other illegal goods. He hires ex-ninja to do his dirty work."

"So why does Gato want you dead?" Kakashi asked.

"About a year ago, he set his sights on the Land of Waves. He used his money and muscle to take over all the ferry boats."

"Sounds like a real sleazeball," Kakashi said. He grimaced and shook his head.

"The Land of Waves is made up of small islands," Tazuna went on. "Whoever controls the ferry boats controls everything."

"But now you and your bridge are in his way," Sakura said thoughtfully. She really was good at grasping situations.

Tazuna nodded at her and continued.

"If we had a bridge, our people wouldn't need Gato's boats. There would be free trade again, without his demands for a piece of the action. So the bridge must be finished."

"Why didn't you tell us before?" Kakashi grumbled. "This assignment is more risky than you let on."

Tazuna sighed.

"The Land of Waves is a very poor country. Even the lords have no money. A B-rank assignment is more than we can afford."

Kakashi and Squad Seven suddenly looked sympathetic,

like they finally understood his situation.

"I know I should have told you," Tazuna said wearily. "But do what you need to do. If you have to leave, I'll understand."

Tazuna saw that the others looked sad, so he tugged on their heartstrings even harder.

"If I die, my grandson will cry all day. But don't you worry about that!" he said pitifully. "If I die, my daughter will hate you forever. But don't worry about that, either!"

Kakashi looked annoyed at first. Then he shrugged his shoulders and sighed.

"Okay, okay. You win. We'll watch over you 'til you get home."

As they all walked away, they heard a ninja yell.

"Hey, you with the silver hair! What do we do now?"

"Whatever you want," Kakashi smoothly replied.

"Huh?"

Kakashi walked back to face him.

"Your next attack will be your last," he said in a low voice. "So tell your boss to back off. He can send a million guys, but it still won't matter."

Kakashi's tone was casual, but the ninja clearly got the message.

"Is everything okay?" Sasuke asked when Kakashi rejoined the group.

"Depends what you mean by okay."

"Shouldn't you kill them?" Sasuke asked earnestly.

"What if they report back to their headquarters?"

"Report?" Kakashi snorted. "Another ninja probably already has. It's useless to shut them up."

"But, but..." Sasuke sputtered, looking back at the ninja.

Kakashi laughed.

"Just leave 'em alone, kid. Okay?"

Sasuke looked miffed but quit talking.

"This is a simple, bare-bones assignment," Kakashi reminded them. "We're not out to kill our fathers' enemies. We just wanna beat up the bad guys."

But even as he spoke, Kakashi's mind was on other things. No one in Squad Seven had ever killed anybody. That day would surely come, but hopefully not for a good long while. At the very least, Kakashi didn't want the blood of punks like that on his students' hands.

Life is so complicated, he thought. He wanted to show them the way of the ninja. But they also needed to know how—and when—to kill an enemy.

"Let's scram before anything else happens," Kakashi said, picking up the pace.

The rest of their journey went well, and they soon reached the port where they would board a ship to the Land of Waves. They steered clear of a passenger vessel owned by Gato, and headed for a remote area.

"My comrade will be waiting here," Tazuna told them.

Sure enough, a small boat was tied up near some

rocks.

"We're all goin' in this little tub?" Naruto scoffed.

Tazuna chuckled.

"Don't worry, the Land of Waves isn't far. I'm building a bridge to there, remember? We just need a nice fog to hide us."

But nature didn't cooperate, so they couldn't leave until the middle of the night. The fog finally showed up at dawn, making everything look as murky as miso soup.

"You'll see the bridge soon," the boatman said tensely.

"Turn off the engine. Gato's guys could be hiding anywhere," Tazuna whispered.

The engine sputtered to a stop. Now the only sound was the quiet *slosh-slosh* of the paddle in the water.

Soon a large gray shadow emerged from the fog.

"Look! It's the bridge!" Sakura whispered in awe.

"Whoa! It's humongous!" Naruto yelled.

The boatman frowned at him.

"Shhh! Quiet down! We're very close to shore."

"S-sorry," Naruto whispered back.

It was slow going without a motor. They were in the boat for nearly an hour before they finally saw land. As the fog started to lift, a stone wall appeared near the shore, cut through with tunnels for boats to pass through.

"The inland waterway is the safest route. That okay with you?" the boatman asked.

Tazuna nodded.

The boatman paddled on. Soon the boat glided through a tunnel and entered a river lined with mangrove trees.

They finally docked at a pier. As soon as the passengers climbed out, the boatman revved up the engine and sped away.

"I'm almost home!" Tazuna said, sounding happy for the first time since they'd met him. "Follow me!"

They started walking down a road that ran along the water. On the other side grew a dense thicket of shrubs. As they walked on, the thicket turned into a shadowy forest of tall trees.

It was the perfect hiding place for enemies.

Naruto had been on high alert since yesterday's brutal attack. Only problem was, now he saw trouble wherever he looked, or at least he thought he did.

"I see you, scum!" he suddenly roared, spinning a shuriken into the woods.

"See who?" Kakashi asked, dumbfounded.

Naruto pointed to the woods uncertainly.

"I...I thought I saw something move over there."

"Don't throw shuriken willy-nilly like that!" Kakashi scolded. "With your skills, it could be dangerous."

But Naruto was already looking for his next target.

"Naruto! Did you hear what sensei said?" Sakura snapped, marching toward him. She had no problem getting on his case for whatever reason.

Just as Sakura was about to pounce, Naruto quickly spun another shuriken.

"Gotcha!" he yelled triumphantly.

Sakura socked Naruto's head with her fist.

"Owww! Cut it out!" Naruto yelled.

"Sensei told you to stop!"

"But there really is something there!" Naruto insisted. He ran into the woods to prove his point. Sadly, he was right.

A soft white rabbit lay dead beside his shuriken.

"Now look what you did!" Sakura said with outrage.

"I-I'm sorry. I didn't mean to..."

Kakashi ignored their noisy squabble as he continued to scan their surroundings. Naruto wasn't completely off-target. Kakashi had sensed something, too.

A snow hare in spring? How strange, he thought.

A rabbit's fur stays white all winter, but when spring arrives, bringing more sun, the fur gradually turns brown.

This rabbit had been kept indoors for some reason. Was it some kind of decoy?

All of a sudden Kakashi sensed some very evil vibes.

"Get down, everybody!" he hollered.

They all hit the ground as an enormous sword buzzed over them. If they had still been standing up, it would have sliced them all in half.

The sword cut into a big tree trunk and stopped moving. A tall guy leaped up and stood on the handle.

Where's his eyebrows? Naruto wondered.

"Ahh! Now I see why the Demon Brothers failed," the guy sneered down at them. His eyes flashed when he saw Kakashi, who was slowly getting up.

"Well! If it isn't the famous copy ninja of the Hidden Leaves! Kakashi and his sharingan."

"Sharingan?" Sasuke gasped.

Kakashi ignored him and looked up at the tall guy.

"Zabuza Momochi, the rogue ninja of the Hidden Mist. Fancy meeting you here."

Naruto was behind Kakashi, ready to rumble.

"Don't, Naruto," Kakashi warned. "He's tougher than those other guys."

"Relax, Kakashi. I have no intention of fighting you," Zabuza said calmly.

He pointed down at Tazuna and sniggered.

"I'm here to kill him."

"Get in Manji battle formation!" Kakashi shouted to his students. "Guard Tazuna!"

Zabuza burst out laughing.

Kakashi looked sharply at Squad Seven.

"You guys stay out of this! Just watch Tazuna!"

He watched to make sure they were listening, then did something truly shocking. Kakashi pulled up his headband to reveal his mysterious left eye.

Naruto had been right. Kakashi was hiding an old scar that ran vertically from his eyebrow to his cheek.

But that wasn't all he was hiding. His left eye had a bright red iris, within which floated three black symbols shaped like commas.

Kakashi stared up at Zabuza.

"Leave the old man alone. You'll have to fight me first."

"Lucky, lucky me!" Zabuza jeered. "I get to see the famous sharingan!"

Kakashi didn't reply, but Zabuza kept on talking.

"When I was in the Anbu Black Ops Unit of the Hidden Mist, you were in our Bingo Book. I hear you've copied more than a thousand jutsu."

Sasuke suddenly tensed up.

He knew the sharingan could see through all jutsu and reflect them back like a mirror. It could also copy any jutsu it saw and add them to a ninja's arsenal of skills.

Sasuke had heard the sharingan only appeared in very special members of the Uchiha Clan. And Kakashi was definitely not a member of the Uchiha Clan.

"Well, enough chit-chat. I have an old geezer to kill," Zabuza said.

Zabuza bent his knees and prepared to jump. Tazuna went deathly pale. Squad Seven stayed in Manji battle formation, their kunai drawn and ready. Kakashi stood in front of Tazuna, not saying a single word. He just kept looking up at Zabuza.

"Move, Kakashi! Or I'll have to kill you first!" Zabuza growled.

Suddenly he vanished with his sword. Seconds later, there was a sound of rushing water. Everybody turned to look. Zabuza stood atop a swift whirlpool, his huge sword strapped to his back. He was already making a sign.

"Ninja Art: Hidden Mist Jutsu!" Zabuza shouted.

A heavy mist rose up from the water's surface. It completely concealed Zabuza, then drifted out to where the others stood. Soon they could barely see each other.

"This guy's a silent killing expert!" Kakashi hollered. "He'll come for me first, but watch out! You could be dead before you know it!"

Squad Seven suddenly looked terrified.

"The fog's getting thicker!" Naruto gasped.

"Listen! Can you hear that?" Sakura said softly.

Zabuza was excitedly whispering something that sounded like a murderer's to-do list.

"Throat, spinal column, lungs, liver, jugular vein, subclavian artery, kidney, and heart! What shall I drill through first?"

He cackled like a witch.

Zabuza's voice echoed eerily through the mist, so they couldn't quite pinpoint where he was. This made Squad Seven feel even more vulnerable.

Then Kakashi made a move. He raised both arms, closed his right eye, and executed a sign. His sharingan was wide open for business.

Suddenly Kakashi looked deadly serious. Squad Seven

had never seen him like that. It gave them goosebumps all over.

Sasuke struggled to breathe the dense air. The two jonin-level ninja emitted an energy so intense he could almost reach out and touch it.

I can't move, or breathe, or even blink an eyelid, Sasuke thought wildly. *If I do, he'll kill me!*

"Sasuke. Calm down," Kakashi suddenly said.

Sasuke looked over at his sensei. Kakashi was about to attack, but he glanced back at Sasuke and smiled.

"Don't worry. I'll protect you guys, even if he gets me," he said reassuringly. "I will never let my comrades die!"

"Is that so?" Zabuza sneered. "How sweet!"

He took a big leap and landed right in the middle of the Manji battle formation. Everybody in Squad Seven looked frantic. What in the world should they do now?

Then Kakashi blew in like a strong wind and pushed them all out of harm's way. He thrust a kunai in Zabuza's stomach, but unfortunately, that didn't end it.

"Sensei! Behind you!" Naruto shrieked.

Kakashi quickly looked back to see yet another Zabuza. As the Zabuza in front of him splashed to the ground, the Zabuza behind him wildly swung his sword. It cut through Kakashi's waist like it was a sushi roll.

Sakura screamed in horror as her sensei was sliced in two. Then something really weird happened. Kakashi's top and bottom halves became liquid, too!

Zabuza couldn't believe his eyes. *A water clone? He copied my jutsu in this fog?*

Suddenly Zabuza felt the cold sharp blade of a kunai against the back of his neck.

"This ends here," Kakashi said ominously.

But Zabuza didn't even wince. He laughed.

"You still don't get it, do you?" he snorted.

Kakashi kept the kunai on his neck while Zabuza kept on babbling.

"Needless to say, I am impressed. You copied my jutsu perfectly, even through this fog!"

Suddenly Kakashi felt someone breathing down his neck.

"But I'm not that easy to fool!" Zabuza snarled from behind.

The Zabuza in front of Kakashi splashed away as the Zabuza behind him swung his sword. Kakashi instantly hit the ground, but the huge blade still grazed his back.

Kakashi tried to get up, but Zabuza was way too fast for him. Zabuza stabbed his sword in the ground, then leaned on the handle and kicked Kakashi's side. Kakashi sailed across the landscape for what seemed like forever, until he finally splashed into a deep puddle.

"Now where's that old geezer?" Zabuza roared. He swaggered toward Tazuna, who was cowering near a tree. All of a sudden Zabuza stopped in his tracks.

Dozens of steel caltrops were scattered across the

ground in front of him. They looked like the toy jacks little girls play with, but their needle-sharp points were dipped in poison.

"What is this? A joke?" Zabuza scoffed. He forgot all about Tazuna and headed straight for Kakashi again.

Kakashi was struggling to get out of the puddle, but the water was holding him down for some reason.

Why is this stuff so heavy? Kakashi wondered.

Zabuza quickly made a sign and chanted a spell.

"Water Prison Jutsu!" he yelled.

Water swirled furiously around Kakashi until he was trapped inside a huge liquid globe. Zabuza thrust his hand inside and wiggled his fingers at the prisoner.

"Thanks for falling into my trap!" he jeered. "I can't do my job if you're running around wild."

Kakashi pushed hard with both hands, but the wall of water held fast.

"You can't escape, so quit trying," Zabuza scoffed. "Now excuse me, I have work to do."

Keeping one hand inside the liquid prison, Zabuza looked at Squad Seven and made a sign with his other hand.

"I'll take care of the kids first," he grunted.

A water clone instantly bobbed up in front of them.

"Little ninja wannabes! Did you think those lame headbands would protect you?" he snickered.

Squad Seven didn't move.

"A real ninja has faced death," the clone growled. "You really wanna be ninja? Then do something that gets my attention. Do something that gets you into my Bingo Book."

The clone disappeared, though they still sensed its presence.

"Where'd he go?" gasped Naruto, looking around nervously. Two seconds later, he found out.

The clone kicked Naruto so hard his headband flew off. As Naruto sailed backward, the clone crunched his headband under his foot. Back at the liquid prison, the real Zabuza watched the scene with relish.

"You're not ninja!" he smirked. "You're just little brats."

"Everybody run!" Kakashi yelled from his watery cell. "And take Tazuna with you!"

Squad Seven looked at Kakashi with fear.

"He won't come after you!" Kakashi assured them. "He has to stay with me! And he can't manipulate the water clone if it's too far away from him."

Naruto was still sprawled on the ground, trembling all over. The clone stood a few feet away, watching and waiting.

I have to escape! Naruto thought feverishly. *If I don't, he'll kill me!*

He tried to get up, but fell back on his left hand, which was still in bandages. As a sharp pain shot up his arm,

Naruto flashed back to a fateful moment. He saw himself stabbing his hand, and remembered what he had solemnly vowed that day.

I will never be rescued again. I will never wuss out again. And I will never, ever let Sasuke show me up like that. I swear all this by the pain of my left hand.

Naruto looked at Zabuza's clone, who was still stomping on his headband. He had given his all to win that badge of ninja honor, and he was not about to stop now.

"Guess what, buster? This time, I'm not running away!" Naruto hollered, dashing recklessly toward the clone and snatching up his headband.

The clone kicked Naruto's small body like it was a playground ball. Naruto swiftly rolled back to the rest of his squad, his headband in his hand.

"What are you doing?" Sakura shrieked. "We can't fight somebody like him! We're only genin!"

Naruto didn't answer. He struggled to his feet, then turned to yell at the real Zabuza.

"Hey, you over there! The guy with no eyebrows!"

Zabuza glared at him, but Naruto didn't back down.

"You better put me in your Bingo Book! Be sure to say I'm the future Hokage of the Hidden Leaf!"

Naruto quickly tied his headband back on.

"Naruto Uzumaki! Leaf-School Ninja!"

A BRILLIANT PLAN

Zabuza kept glaring at Naruto.

"You're pretty full of yourself, runt!" he sneered. "Do you really think you can beat me?"

"I told you guys to run!" Kakashi hollered. "Your only job is to protect Tazuna, remember?"

Kakashi knew his students were in peril. Even if they worked as a team, they were still no match for Zabuza.

There was something else to consider. Tazuna had hired them as his guards. And a ninja's assignment always came first, no matter what.

Naruto knew all that, but he also knew they had to save their sensei. He looked back at Tazuna with a question in his eyes.

Tazuna instantly got the message.

"Go get him, kids!" he yelled.

"Thanks!" Naruto shouted, and swung around to face the clone. Sasuke stepped up next to him. Sakura hesitated for a second, but quickly joined her comrades.

"Listen! I've got a plan!" Naruto whispered to Sasuke.

"You mean teamwork?" Sasuke whispered back.

Zabuza laughed like it was the funniest joke he'd ever heard.

"Still playin' ninja, huh? Don't you kiddies ever learn?"

"What's wrong with that?" Naruto snarled. "We can't lose against you!"

"You can't win either. You punks have never even killed anybody," Zabuza said coldly. "When I was your age, my hands were already stained with blood."

Naruto and the others shivered. Were they really about to slaughter their first enemy?

"Now I remember! You're Zabuza...the demon!" Kakashi suddenly hissed from his liquid prison.

"So! You've heard of me!" Zabuza chortled.

"The Hidden Mist Village has been called the Blood Mist Village, and for good reason," Kakashi muttered. "Once upon a time they had a brutal ninja initiation rite."

"Ahh! You've heard about our graduation exam," Zabuza said with an evil chuckle.

"What graduation exam?" Naruto piped up.

Zabuza looked down at the ground and laughed.

"C'mon, tell us!" Naruto demanded.

Zabuza kept on laughing. When he finally looked up, there was madness in his eyes.

"The students had to kill each other."

"Wh-what do you mean?" Naruto stammered. Sakura and Sasuke looked shocked.

Zabuza didn't bother to answer, so Kakashi explained the grisly ritual.

"They divided the students into pairs, then forced them to fight until one of them died. These were comrades who had studied together, shared their dreams with each other, eaten from the same pot of rice..."

"But that's...that's awful!" Sakura shuddered.

Kakashi nodded bitterly before he continued.

"Ten years ago, something horrible happened which finally forced them to change their ways."

"What?" Sakura asked anxiously.

Kakashi paused and lowered his voice.

"A boy who didn't even qualify as a ninja massacred every one of the applicants. He killed over one hundred students."

"Now that was a fun time!" Zabuza sniggered.

He glared at Squad Seven with murder in his eyes. His urge to kill them was so strong they could almost feel it.

Sasuke never even saw him coming. Quick as a flash, the clone jabbed Sasuke's ribs with his elbow and punched his face with his fist. He slammed Sasuke to the ground and stepped on his chest.

"Sasuke!" Sakura screamed.

Blood spurted from Sasuke's mouth, but the clone still

wasn't finished with him. He glared down at his prey as he reached back for his sword.

"Now you die," he muttered.

"You wish!" Naruto shrieked, quickly making a sign.

Seconds later, the clone was surrounded by a gang of Narutos. But he was far from impressed.

"My, my. Just look at all the shadow clones," he sneered.

The Narutos gripped their kunai and went for the clone's head. The clone was soon lost inside a mob of angry twelve-year-olds.

Sasuke seized the opportunity to escape, and not a moment too soon. Zabuza's clone swung his sword in a big circle, scattering the Naruto clones far and wide.

They vanished one by one, leaving just the real Naruto behind. He quickly took off his backpack, then reached inside to pull out a stack of four long blades welded to a ring-shaped handle.

"Sasuke! Heads up!" Naruto shouted, flinging the weapon in his direction.

Sasuke caught the heavy blades by their ring.

So that's what Naruto has in mind, he thought. *Excellent.*

Sasuke staggered backward but kept a tight grip on the handle. With a quick snap of his wrist, the blades unfolded like a fan—and became a giant shuriken!

"Demon Wind Shuriken, Windmill of Shadows!" Sasuke yelled, leaping high above the clone Zabuza.

"Tsk! Shuriken can't hurt me!"

But Sasuke wasn't aiming for the clone. The giant shuriken zoomed right for the real Zabuza, who was still holding Kakashi captive.

"Well! About time you went after the real me," Zabuza snorted, grabbing the shuriken by its center hole.

Suddenly a second windmill shuriken appeared in the wake of the first one. Zabuza actually looked shocked for a second. But he quickly jumped up, and the shuriken soared beneath him.

"Nice try, you little weasel," he sneered, turning his attention back to Kakashi.

Bad move on Zabuza's part! He completely missed the main event—when the second shuriken became a boy with blond hair!

"Take this!" Naruto yelled, hurling his kunai with all his might.

Zabuza was caught completely off guard. Both of his hands were occupied: one held the first shuriken, the other was still inside the liquid prison. There was only one thing left to do.

Zabuza pulled his arm out of the water and wildly twisted his body. The kunai lightly grazed his cheek.

"You monster!" he hollered.

Zabuza quickly spun around and aimed the shuriken at Naruto. Suddenly his arm froze into place. He looked back to see Kakashi, who was blocking the blade with his fist.

Kakashi just glared at Zabuza, who gasped with shock.

"That was brilliant, Naruto!" Kakashi shouted. "You guys are really growing up fast."

"Thanks, sensei!" Naruto said proudly. "It was a piece of cake!"

Maybe not *that* easy, but his plan had been clever indeed. One shadow clone had stood in for Naruto as he transformed into a second Demon Wind Shuriken. Sasuke had caught both shuriken and thrown them at Zabuza, leaving the door wide open for Naruto to attack him from behind.

Zabuza still wouldn't admit he'd been tricked.

"Crap! I got so mad I broke my own spell," he whined.

"You didn't break your spell. We did," Kakashi said.

Zabuza glowered at him.

"The same jutsu won't work on me twice," Kakashi said calmly. "Now what will you do?"

All of a sudden, Zabuza and Kakashi jumped away from each other and started making identical signs. The water quickly surged around them like a kettle boiling over.

"Water Style: Water Dragon Jutsu!" they yelled in unison.

Two enormous water dragons sprang up, snapping their jaws at each other. They twisted together to form a geyser as tall as a fir tree. Then it collapsed without warning, splashing water over everything and everybody.

Zabuza lunged toward Kakashi with his sword. Kakashi lunged toward Zabuza with his kunai.

Something's wrong here! Zabuza thought with confusion. *What's going on?*

Like some crazy dance, the two jumped away from each other again at precisely the same time. They circled around in the water, then stopped to make another identical sign.

Zabuza was truly bewildered. He knew Kakashi was copying his jutsu. But Kakashi's signs should have lagged behind his own, if only for a second or two.

He must be reading my mind! Zabuza suddenly thought.

"Yup! I sure am!" Kakashi said out loud.

Zabuza almost gagged, but quickly pulled himself together.

"Pfft! You're just a pale imitation of me!" he scoffed.

"I'm the genuine article! You don't stand a chance!" Kakashi mocked. "Is that what you were gonna say?"

Zabuza instantly went ballistic. His eyes popped out of his head as he furiously made signs. When he saw that Kakashi was copying him, he moved his fingers even faster.

Suddenly Zabuza saw an incredible sight. Was that really him standing behind Kakashi?

"It can't be!" Zabuza gasped. "Must be one of his illusions!"

He got so shook up he stopped making signs, but

Kakashi kept on going.

"Water Style: Giant Vortex Jutsu!" Kakashi shouted.

"Wh-what's happening?" Zabuza stuttered as he watched the sharingan spin.

Zabuza looked astounded as a wall of water surged toward him. The big wave carried him off until he slammed into a distant tree.

"This is it, Zabuza," someone said from above.

Zabuza jerked up his head. Kakashi was kneeling on a high branch, staring down at him.

"Why? You a fortune-teller or something?" Zabuza sneered.

"Yeah. I predict you're gonna die," Kakashi replied, aiming his kunai.

Just then, two long silver needles came shooting out of nowhere and pierced Zabuza's neck. He slowly crumpled, then fell forward with a thud, right on his miserable face.

"Your prediction came true," a voice said from above. "He's dead."

A boy stood atop another tree, wearing a white mask that completely covered his face. It had a swirl painted near the mouth that looked like a fishhook turned sideways.

His black hair was tucked into a small skullcap, except for two long locks that framed his face. He wore a loose robe cinched at the waist by a long sash.

Kakashi watched him spin down from his high perch and land near Zabuza's lifeless body.

"He really is dead," Kakashi whispered in awe.

The boy politely bowed to him.

"Thank you for your help. Hope you don't mind, but I wanted to kill him myself."

"That mask looks familiar," Kakashi said thoughtfully. "Are you a tracker ninja of the Hidden Mist?"

"Yes," the boy admitted. "We hunt down rogue ninja."

The boy sensed someone nearby and turned to see Naruto glaring at him.

"Just who are you anyway?" Naruto snapped.

"Relax, Naruto. He's not an enemy," Kakashi assured him.

"That's not what I mean!" Naruto insisted. He pointed at dead Zabuza.

"How could a kid like him defeat a guy like that? It makes no sense!" Naruto protested. "He made us look like total fools out there."

"I get how you feel, Naruto," Kakashi said. "But that's just the way the world is."

He kindly patted Naruto's head before he continued.

"You know something? There will always be kids who are younger than you, and kids who are stronger than me."

Naruto turned away and sulked.

The boy in the mask watched Naruto and Kakashi with interest. Then he hoisted Zabuza's corpse to his shoulders.

"Now I must dispose of him," he said to no one in particular. "This body holds many secrets..."

He spun away as swiftly as he had arrived.

Kakashi took a deep breath and pulled his headband down to its usual position, over his left eye.

"Let's get Tazuna home before anything else happens!" he said, taking a lively step forward.

His body started swaying from side to side.

"Sensei!" Sakura gasped as Kakashi toppled to the ground.

"That's what I get for using too much sharingan," Kakashi said ruefully.

NINJA IN THE TREES

In the end, Tazuna carried Kakashi all the way home on his back. Luckily, it wasn't too far.

Tazuna lived in a tidy, two-story house that stood on stilts at the edge of the sea. It had a deck outside where you could sit and watch the boats sail by. He shared this home with Tsunami, his grown-up daughter, and her little son.

As soon as they walked in, Tsunami immediately took charge, helping Kakashi to a futon on the floor.

"Are you all right, sensei?" she asked with concern.

"No. But I will be in about a week."

"Gee. I never knew the sharingan could be so hard on your body," Sakura said with wonder.

Kakashi smiled wryly.

"Yeah, well. Nothing I can do about that."

Tazuna had already collapsed, worn out from hauling Kakashi. He chuckled as he wiped the sweat from his face.

"Thanks to you, we should be safe for a while."

"Who was the kid in the mask?" Sakura asked Kakashi.

"He's a tracker ninja from the Hidden Mist Village. They call them the Undertaker Squad."

"Undertaker Squad?" Sakura shuddered. The very name gave her the creeps.

"They kill rogue ninja and completely destroy their corpses, right down to their fingernails."

"But why?" Naruto asked earnestly.

Kakashi gazed up at the ceiling.

"A ninja's body stores many secrets," he explained. "Secrets about ninjutsu, secrets about medicine, even secrets about using chakra."

Everybody listened intently.

"For example, if a ninja took my remains, he would thoroughly study my sharingan. Worse yet, he might even figure out how to copy it."

The members of Squad Seven looked pensive. This was almost more than they cared to know, but they kept on listening.

"That's why corpses must be completely destroyed," Kakashi continued. "So their secrets are never revealed."

Kakashi closed his eyes. When he spoke again, he whispered.

"No sound, no smell. That's how a ninja dies."

Everybody sat in silence for a while, thinking about what Kakashi had said. Suddenly Sakura made a face.

"So he's gonna cut Zabuza up and throw away the pieces? Yyyuck!"

Meanwhile, in the forest, a heavy fog had settled in. The boy in the mask gazed down at dead Zabuza. Beside the body were his tools, neatly stashed in a carrying case. They glowed with an eerie black luster.

"First, I cut off his mask," the boy murmured, picking up some scissors that had seen better days.

Suddenly someone gripped his arm.

"That's enough, Haku. I can do it myself," Zabuza croaked. He pulled down his mask in slow motion.

"What? You're awake already?"

"Of course I am," Zabuza snapped. "You're about as gentle as a butcher." He roughly yanked a needle from his neck.

"Careful, sir! Or you really will die!" Haku warned.

Zabuza glared at him.

"Why are you still wearing that stupid mask? Take it off!" he grumbled.

Haku giggled as he removed it.

"Old habits die hard, I guess. But it was useful today."

The face that emerged was as lovely as a geisha's, with snow white skin and delicate features.

"I got there just in time, you know," Haku went on. "They were about to do you in."

"Why did you aim for my neck?" Zabuza griped. "If

you wanted me in a temporary death state, you should have picked a safer spot."

He hacked up some blood and spit it on the ground. Then he glared back at Haku, who kept on smiling.

"And risk scarring your beautiful body?" Haku joked. "Besides, the neck has smaller muscles. It's easier to hit pressure points."

"Excuses, excuses," Zabuza grumbled.

Haku put away his tools.

"Most people take ages to recover from something like this," he said brightly. "But a strong warrior like you will get better in no time!"

Zabuza's harsh face suddenly softened.

"You really are innocent, Haku. I guess that's why I like you."

"Well, I'm only a kid," Haku said, beaming.

Haku stood up and looked at the sea, which could be seen beyond the thicket.

"Looks like the fog's cleared up."

The thick mist had finally burned off, and the sea sparkled with sunlight.

"Will you be okay next time?" Haku asked.

"Yeah," Zabuza grunted. "Next time, I'll see through that sharingan."

Back at Tazuna's house, Kakashi had been dozing peacefully when he suddenly jolted awake.

"Sensei? Are you okay?" Tsunami asked, jumping to her feet. She had been sitting by the window while Kakashi slept.

"No. Something's wrong."

"Like what?" Naruto piped up. He was sitting on the floor nearby with the rest of his team.

"Usually the Undertaker Squads get rid of corpses on the spot."

"So?" said Sakura, looking puzzled.

"Don't you get it, Sakura? How did that boy get rid of Zabuza's body?"

"How should I know? He took it with him, remember?"

Sakura snapped back.

"Right. But he only needed Zabuza's head to prove that he killed him."

Kakashi gazed up at the ceiling and thoughtfully stroked his chin.

"And what about his weapons? Very unusual, to say the least."

Kakashi was talking about senbon, the long thin needles that are also used in acupuncture. Senbon are only lethal if they hit certain vital body parts.

Sasuke had been quietly listening, but now he suddenly looked astonished.

"No way!" he choked.

"There's a very distinct possibility," Kakashi sighed.

Just then Tazuna spoke up.

"What the heck are you two talking about?" he asked with confusion.

"Zabuza," Kakashi said simply. "We think he's still alive."

Everybody gasped with horror.

"But you said he was dead, sensei!" Sakura shrieked.

"You checked to make sure, remember?" Naruto yelled.

"He looked like a goner to me," Kakashi said. "But that boy probably put him into a death trance."

"Really? How?" Naruto asked with interest. Now there was a skill that could come in handy someday.

"Undertaker Squads know all about the human body. A tracker ninja could easily fake a death scene."

Kakashi tugged on his blanket and continued.

"That boy did two things to make me think Zabuza's still with us. One, he hauled away his body, which must have weighed a ton. Two, he used senbon, which are not always lethal weapons. So the real truth is..."

Kakashi paused to look at them.

"He didn't come to kill Zabuza. He came to help him."

Tazuna sighed and shook his head.

"Maybe you worry too much," he suggested.

"I don't think so," Kakashi said seriously. "Shinobi always consider the worst case scenario. Gato might hire ninja even meaner than Zabuza."

Naruto was shaking with fury. He had risked his life to take down Zabuza, and now the scumbag was still alive?

"You guys can train while I recover," Kakashi decided.

"More training?" Sakura asked doubtfully. "But there's no way we can beat someone like Zabuza."

"Hey, who rescued me from him? You're all improving quickly. Especially you, Naruto."

Naruto's face lit up with joy.

"Just don't expect too much," Kakashi warned. "One week of training won't make you jonin. And three genin are still no match for one stinker like Zabuza."

Sakura looked at Kakashi with anxiety.

"Say Zabuza is still alive," she said. "What if he attacks

us before you can move?"

"It takes a good long while to recover from a death trance. At least I hope it does."

"So we train until he gets better!" Naruto said, jumping to his feet. "Boy, this is really gettin' interesting!"

"Not really," a small voice said.

Everyone turned to see a little boy standing in the doorway. He wore a hat that looked like an upside-down flowerpot with stripes.

"Inari! Where have you been?" Tazuna cried with joy.

Inari took off his shoes and came inside.

"Welcome home, Grandpa," he said quietly.

Inari ran toward Tazuna and hugged him, then shyly hid behind his back.

"Where are your manners, Inari? Say hello to our guests!" Tsunami reminded her son.

Inari peeked at the visitors.

"But, Mama! They're all gonna die!" he protested.

"Wh-what did you say?" Naruto sputtered.

Inari looked at him with eyes older than his years.

"You can't fight Gato and win," he said.

"How do you know?" Naruto scoffed. "I'm gonna be a hero someday, a hokage! That Gato guy is no match for me!"

Inari looked at Naruto with wide eyes. Then he snorted with disgust.

"There's no such thing as a hero," he said.

"You brat! Take that back right now, or else!"

"Leave him alone, Naruto!" Sakura snapped. "He's just a little kid."

"Go home soon if you don't wanna die," Inari said before he took off for his room. Naruto dashed after him.

Upstairs, he heard muffled sounds coming from behind a closed door. Naruto put his ear up to listen. Inari was definitely inside.

"I've got somethin' to say to you," Naruto snapped, sliding the door open.

Inari was looking out the window, crying his heart out. He didn't even hear Naruto enter.

"Daddy...Daddy..." he sobbed.

Naruto hung his head in shame and tiptoed away.

That afternoon, Kakashi took Squad Seven into the forest near Tazuna's home. He was healing fast and could now get around on crutches.

"Today we start chakra training."

"Sensei? What's chakra?" Naruto asked dumbly.

Kakashi sighed and slumped his shoulders.

"Go ahead, Sakura. Tell him."

"Chakra: the fuel a ninja uses while doing a jutsu," she said, sounding like a dictionary. "It's a combination of physical and mental energy."

"Oh, yeah," Naruto said. "I always fell asleep when the sensei taught us stuff like that."

Sakura groaned and rolled her eyes.

"So what's the big deal?" Naruto groused. "We don't need that to do jutsu."

"Naruto's right," Sasuke chimed in. "We can still do jutsu, even if we don't know about chakra."

But Kakashi shook his head.

"Not true. Every ninja needs to learn how to use chakra effectively," he explained.

Kakashi adjusted his crutches and continued.

"Like Sakura said, chakra is a mixture of physical and mental energy, but the balance is never the same. Each jutsu requires a different recipe. If you don't follow the right recipe, a jutsu could blow up in your face. You wind up wasting time and energy."

Naruto looked dazed. Listening was never his strong suit, but he was trying to follow along.

"So, uh, how do we learn all that?" he asked.

"This week you'll practice controlling chakra with your body. But I'm warning you, this training is very hard and very risky."

They all looked a little nervous. Just what did Kakashi have in mind?

"Your first lesson will be climbing trees," he said.

"C-climbing trees?" Sakura gulped.

"Yup. Climbing trees without using your hands."

"What?"

"Just watch, okay?"

Kakashi hobbled over to a nearby cedar. He quickly made a sign and planted his foot on the trunk. Then he walked up the tree as easily as he walked on land, when he wasn't injured, that is.

When Kakashi came to a branch, he kept on walking, except now he was upside down!

When he was halfway across, Kakashi paused to glance down at Squad Seven. They looked like three little birds with their beaks wide open.

"Use your chakra well, and you can do this, too," he promised.

"You w-w-want us to do that?" Sakura asked shakily.

Kakashi squinted down at her.

"It's tricky," he admitted. "You need just the right amount of chakra to stick to the trunk. Even veteran ninja have trouble sometimes."

Kakashi pointed to his feet.

"The soles of your feet are two of the hardest places to focus your chakra on. But if you can learn to do that, you can learn to do anything."

"Can we get started?" Naruto said impatiently. He was raring to go, but the lecture wasn't over.

"A ninja also needs to know how to maintain a constant level of chakra for long periods of time," Kakashi went on. "This skill is even harder to learn."

"Got it!" Naruto snapped. "Can we practice now?"

"One more thing. A ninja can't stop fighting just to fix

his chakra. He or she must adjust his chakra on the fly, in the heat of battle."

"So that's why we're climbing trees?" Sakura asked.

"Yup! It's the best way to learn about chakra control."

He threw three kunai at the ground near their feet.

"Climb as high as you can, and stick the kunai into the trunk at that spot. Each time you go up, move the marker a little higher. Okay?"

Naruto was first to grab a kunai.

"I can do this easy!" he boasted. "I'm improving the most, after all!"

"Enough big talk, Naruto. Just do it."

Naruto imitated Kakashi's sign and concentrated for a moment. Then he dashed to the tree with fighting spirit.

Too much fighting spirit, as it turned out. He took one step on the trunk and immediately flopped backward. Naruto's feet refused to stick because he didn't focus enough chakra.

Sasuke, on the other hand, focused way too much. His feet didn't stick to the trunk, but were actually repelled. He only managed a few steps up before he flopped down next to Naruto.

As they sprawled in the dirt, grumbling, they heard a familiar giggle from above.

"Hey! This is pretty easy!"

Naruto and Sasuke looked up. Sakura gaily waved down at them from a high branch.

"Check it out, boys!" Kakashi said. "Now there's a girl who can really control her chakra! Nice work, Sakura!"

Kakashi was pleased at Sakura's progress, but he knew it was something of a fluke. Both Naruto and Sasuke had more chakra at their disposal than Sakura ever would.

Now if they can just learn how to control it, Kakashi thought hopefully.

As Squad Seven kept practicing, they didn't see a little boy watching from behind a tree.

"Just wasting their time," Inari muttered.

He turned and ran all the way home.

HEROES AND VILLAINS

The next day, Gato showed up at the secret cabin shaped like a pine tree.

He didn't bother to knock. His samurai kicked in the door for him. Gato barreled inside to find Zabuza in bed, with Haku sitting beside him.

"They beat you at your own game, Zabuza!" Gato bellowed. "If you ask me, you Mist ninja are pretty second-rate."

Haku glared at the uninvited guests, while Zabuza just gazed at the ceiling.

Gato stood with a samurai on either side, looking like a bonsai between two redwoods. One samurai was shirtless and covered with tattoos, while the other wore a winter coat and hat. Both carried long swords, which they obviously knew how to use. But no matter how big their swords were, most samurai still couldn't compete with ninja fighting skills.

"You call yourself a demon?" Gato sneered. "Don't make me laugh. You couldn't even clean up after the Demon Brothers."

Zabuza kept gazing at the ceiling.

The samurai grabbed their swords and stepped forward. Zabuza's aloof attitude was really starting to bug them.

"Back off," Gato barked, creeping closer to the bed. He leaned over and reached for Zabuza's hand.

"Say something, will you?" Gato snarled. Suddenly he shrieked with pain and glared down at his wrist.

Haku was gripping it so tightly, Gato could almost hear his bones break. How could a young boy be so strong?

"Don't touch him with your dirty hands," Haku said in a threatening tone.

"Owwww! Let gooo!" Gato begged.

The samurai hurried to his side.

One instant later, Haku was holding their own swords against their necks. The samurai looked absolutely stunned.

"Did you see him move?" one gasped.

"No! He must be a monster!" gasped the other.

"Now I'm really angry," Haku said. He glared at Gato with murder in his eyes.

If looks could kill, Gato was definitely dead meat. He would remember Haku's eyes until the day he died.

Gato just stood there, sweating and shaking, until he finally found the strength to speak.

"Screw up again and you're out of here!" he yelped. "You'll have to find another secret hideout!"

He and the samurai stomped away, slamming the door behind them.

"You shouldn't have gotten him all riled up like that," Zabuza said, putting down his kunai. He had secretly grabbed it while Gato was there.

"I know," Haku admitted. "We can't kill Gato yet, or they could find us again. Let's just lie low for now."

"Okay," Zabuza agreed.

These rogue ninja of the Hidden Mist had found sanctuary in the forest. But if the real tracker ninja got wind of their whereabouts, there would be no escape.

The next day brought clear skies. At the bridge, Tazuna was working hard when he suddenly saw Sakura. She was leaning against a railing, yawning with boredom.

"All alone?" he asked. "Where's that blond kid and the one who puts on airs?"

"Still training," Sakura told him. "I already beat them, so sensei said to guard you."

"You beat them? Really?" Tazuna said with surprise.

So he's one of them, Sakura thought peevishly. *The kind who thinks girls can't be ninja.*

Kakashi really had told Sakura to come here. Someone had to guard the bridge builder until Kakashi got back on his feet.

A man of Tazuna's age approached, looking troubled.

"Tazuna? Can we talk?" he asked.

"What's wrong, Giichi?"

"I've, uh, been thinking things over," Giichi began.

"Don't tell me you're quitting, too?" Tazuna gasped.

"I know we go back a long way, Tazuna. But Gato isn't just after you. He's after us all."

Tazuna didn't answer. He'd heard this all before.

"C'mon, Tazuna! Is this bridge really worth it?"

"Yes," Tazuna said with conviction. "We need this bridge to save our country."

He sighed and wiped the sweat from his forehead.

"But I understand, Giichi. Do what you think is best."

Giichi hurried away before Tazuna changed his mind.

"Enough for today," Tazuna sighed. "Let's go, ninja girl."

They left the bridge and hiked to a nearby village. Sakura felt uneasy as soon as they got there.

"What's with this place? The shops are all empty," she whispered to Tazuna.

She glanced nervously at a raggedy young man with a sign. "I need a job," it said.

"Stop, thief!" another man hollered. He was chasing a frightened little boy who clutched a small bag of rice.

As they walked on, the scene grew even more depressing. Little kids crouched in the dirt, resting their heads on their hands. One grubby young girl ran up to

Sakura looking desperate.

"Got anything to eat?" she begged.

All Sakura had was candy she kept for emergencies, but she gave all of it to the little girl. In an instant, beggars of all ages swooped down on her like vultures.

"Go away!" Sakura yelled.

They scurried off like rats. So did the little girl.

"What's wrong with this town?" Sakura shuddered.

"It's been like this since Gato got here. Everybody's turned into jellyfish."

Tazuna stopped walking and dreamily looked off into the distance.

"We need the bridge as a symbol of our courage," he said quietly. "The people of the Land of Waves should never bow down to anybody."

Sakura didn't know what to say.

Back in the forest, Sasuke was making progress. After just one day, he could climb almost as high as Kakashi.

Naruto was progressing, too. At first, he couldn't climb at all, but now he was nearly at Sasuke's level.

There was a secret to Naruto's success, however. Yesterday he had swallowed his pride to ask Sakura for help, even though he was terrified she'd make fun of him.

Sakura's advice was pure and simple.

"Easy does it, Naruto. Just relax and focus on the tree."

Naruto usually charged full speed ahead, no matter what the situation. "Easy does it" was a brand-new concept for him. But to his surprise, it actually seemed to work!

Even Sasuke had noticed his improvement.

He's almost as good as me, he thought with irritation.

Naruto felt irritated, too. No matter how hard he tried, he still couldn't catch up to Sasuke.

"Hey, Naruto!" Sasuke suddenly yelled.

Naruto was so startled he slipped and fell on his face.

"Do you mind? I'm tryin' to concentrate here!" he snapped.

Sasuke looked sheepish, like he was too embarrassed to speak. Finally he opened his mouth.

"Uh, can I ask you something? What did Sakura say to you?" he said in a rush.

Naruto looked blank for a second. Hold on! Did the great Sasuke just ask *him* for help? Yep, he did!

"I'm not tellin'!" Naruto said with a big grin.

Sasuke just snorted at him.

Naruto and Sasuke practiced climbing until it got dark. When they returned to Tazuna's, supper was ready and waiting for them. They gobbled everything in sight and kept on gobbling.

"I know you two wanna beat each other," Kakashi said wryly. "But eating 'til you puke is just stupid."

Sakura had already finished her plate and was wandering around the room.

"Hey! Who's missing here?" she asked, pointing to a photograph on the wall.

It was a Tazuna family portrait, but one member had obviously been torn out of the picture.

Everybody kept on eating. Finally Tsunami spoke.

"That was my husband," she said curtly.

"He used to be the town hero," Tazuna said.

Inari jumped up and bolted for the door.

"Inari! Where are you going?" Tsunami called after him.

Inari ignored her and went outside. Tsunami glared at her father.

"I told you not to talk about him in front of Inari!" she snapped.

"What's this all about?" Kakashi asked. He sounded as casual as ever, but he was definitely fishing for information.

Tazuna sighed.

"It all started three years ago," he began. While the others listened intently, Tazuna told the whole sad story.

Inari had lost his father when he was very small. Since then, like Naruto, he'd been picked on by the other kids.

The village bullies loved to throw his dog Poochie into the sea. One day their teasing took a tragic turn.

"Hey, Inari! Your dumb dog's drowning! Better go get him!" the bullies jeered. Inari couldn't swim, but they still pushed him into the water.

He sank straight to the bottom and didn't even try to

save himself. Soon he lost consciousness.

When Inari came to, he was wrapped in warm blankets in front of a roaring campfire. A kind young fisherman named Kaiza had rescued him.

"Here, eat!" he told Inari, handing him a fish he had roasted on a stick.

"I tried to save Poochie!" Inari whimpered. "B-but I couldn't!"

Kaiza tenderly patted his head.

"Of course you couldn't," he said softly. "You're just a little boy."

His words made Inari feel better. So did the roasted fish. They ate quietly for a while until Kaiza spoke again.

"When you become a man, you have to walk a straight road that won't leave you filled with regrets," he said.

Inari wasn't sure what that meant, but he liked listening to the nice man.

"If something is precious to you, you must protect it with your life!" Kaiza declared. "Even if you die in the attempt, at least the world will know you tried! That would be your legacy!"

Suddenly Kaiza chuckled.

"Sorry, kid! I kinda get carried away sometimes!"

"Yeah!" Inari said, grinning from ear to ear.

From that moment on, Kaiza was Inari's hero. They saw each other every single day. Inari started to walk like Kaiza, talk like Kaiza, and even spike up his hair like Kaiza.

At first, Tsunami was just glad Inari had made a friend. After a while, her feelings for Kaiza grew deeper. Soon Kaiza became one of the family, which made Inari even happier.

Before long, Kaiza had become a hero to the whole village.

When there was a flood, he closed the dam to contain the damage. When there was a quarrel between towns, he stepped up to settle things. When the nets turned up empty, he searched for new fishing grounds. When storms soaked the fields with salt, he went to faraway places to bring back fresh soil.

In the past, the villagers thought such feats were impossible, so they had never even bothered to try. But Kaiza proved them wrong over and over again.

Inari was proud of this man he called father. Even the villagers started to believe the impossible might actually be possible.

Then Gato arrived in the Land of Waves and wanted everything he laid his eyes on. His greedy tentacles soon reached out to their village, too.

One day Kaiza decided it was time to act. Though Tazuna and Tsunami tried to stop him, he went off alone to meet with Gato, hoping to strike a deal.

The next day, Gato and his samurai came to town. As the villagers watched with horror, the samurai erected a large wooden post on the plaza. They tied a man to the post, someone the villagers knew well.

It was Kaiza, of course.

They whipped Kaiza until his body bled, but his eyes still looked determined. Though weak with pain, Kaiza searched out Inari in the crowd and gave him a special smile.

"Daddy! Daddy!" Inari yelled at the top of his voice.

Gato sneered when he heard the child scream.

"This man is a terrorist!" Gato told the crowd. "He threatened me and my company! There's only one punishment for that!"

The crowd waited with baited breath, but they knew in their hearts what was coming next.

"Public execution!" Gato roared.

The crowd all gasped, but Inari was too young to understand what those words actually meant.

"Daddy! Daddy!" he kept shouting until his throat was raw and sore.

This time, the impossible did not become possible.

As Gato smugly watched, his samurai unsheathed a long sword and lunged at Kaiza. Seconds later, bright red blood streamed over the plaza—and Kaiza was dead.

"Inari's changed since then," Tazuna sighed. "So have the rest of us."

So that's why he acts that way, Naruto thought.

"Inari threw out every single memento he had of his father, including his picture," Tazuna said sadly. "It was the only way he could heal."

Naruto suddenly felt restless, but when he tried to get up, he fell back in his chair.

"No more training today, Naruto," Kakashi said sternly. "If you work any harder, you'll die."

"I don't care. I'm gonna prove it to him."

"Huh?"

Everybody looked at Naruto, who was finally standing.

"I'm gonna prove there are still heroes left in this world," Naruto vowed. Then he left the room.

A GIRL IN THE FOREST

The days passed by.

Naruto practiced tree-climbing almost continuously. He only went back to Tazuna's for meals. Sometimes he even slept in the forest.

Despite Kakashi's warnings, Naruto didn't train himself to death. In fact, Kakashi was amazed by his incredible stamina. The marks on the tree trunk crept higher and higher.

Soon it was the sixth morning of training.

"Naruto didn't come home again last night," Tsunami worried. "Are you sure he's okay?"

Kakashi smiled.

"He's fine," he assured her. "He may not look it, but he's a full-fledged ninja."

Inari was busy scribbling something at the table, but he glanced up every time they mentioned Naruto.

"I wonder. Maybe he really is dead," Sasuke said.

Inari's face fell.

"Nah! He's just passed out on the forest floor like always," Kakashi chuckled.

But Inari still looked upset.

Kakashi was right. The bright morning sun was shining through the trees, but Naruto kept on sleeping. He looked so peaceful even the birds weren't afraid, and pecked around his body for food.

"You'll catch cold sleeping here," a soft voice said.

Naruto felt a hand on his shoulder. He opened his eyes and saw a girl beaming at him. She had snow white skin and was as pretty as a geisha.

"Who...Who are you?" he asked sleepily.

The girl flipped back her long black hair and showed him a basket filled with grasses.

"I've been picking medicinal herbs," she said. "Someone I know is sick."

"This early in the morning? You've been busy, girl!"

"Looks like you've been busy, too. Why are you here at this hour?"

"Who, me? I was training!" Naruto said proudly.

"Oh! I thought you looked like a ninja," she said.

"Really? Do I?" Naruto bubbled. "As a matter of fact, I am!"

He leaned closer to her. No stranger had ever called him a ninja before.

The girl giggled and kept smiling at him.

"You must be a very interesting person. Why are you training?"

"To get stronger!" Naruto said, flexing his biceps. "I'm gonna be the best ninja in my village someday."

"Gee. You look so big and strong already," the girl cooed.

"Nah! I hafta to be a lot stronger than this," Naruto said. "I have something to prove to somebody."

Suddenly the girl stopped smiling.

"Are you training for yourself—or someone else?"

"What do you mean?" Naruto asked, puzzled.

She giggled again.

"Is there someone special in your life?"

Naruto still looked baffled, so she tried to explain.

"When people have someone special to protect, that often makes them stronger."

"Oh, yeah! Now I see what you mean," Naruto said.

He thought about the bond between Inari and Kaiza, and the way sensei always looked after their students.

But before he could speak, the girl abruptly stood up with her basket.

"Sorry to interrupt your practice," she apologized. "You will get stronger, you know. Hope we meet again."

She started walking away, then stopped and looked back.

"By the way, I'm a boy."

Haku had ditched the mask and let down his hair, but he was still the guy who tricked them into believing Zabuza was dead.

Naruto didn't realize that, however. His mind was on something else entirely.

A boy? But he's even more girly than Sakura!

The next morning, Kakashi and Sakura went to the forest training ground. Kakashi was getting around much better now, but still needed a crutch to lean on. When they arrived, Naruto and Sasuke were nowhere to be seen.

"What now?" Kakashi groaned. "Don't tell me they stopped training."

"Look at me, sensei!" someone yelled from above.

Naruto waved down from a high perch.

"I can climb way up here now!" he bragged.

Never one to miss a chance to show off, Naruto stood on the branch and jumped for joy. Suddenly he slipped.

"Nooooo!" Kakashi gasped, hobbling to the tree as fast as he could.

Turns out Naruto didn't need saving after all.

"Fooled ya!" he chortled down at them.

Kakashi and Sakura gaped up in amazement. Naruto was hanging upside down like a bat, with both feet stuck to the branch. It was the same pose Kakashi had struck on the first day of training.

Sakura had been terrified for Naruto. Now she was

hopping mad.

"You idiot!" she shrieked. "Why'd you do that?"

"Heee! You should see the look on your face!" Naruto howled. "I really surprised...ooops!"

This time he wasn't joking. Once Naruto's feet were off the branch, there was no way to stick them back again, no matter how much he focused his chakra.

As Kakashi and Sakura watched with terror, Naruto started a headlong dive to his death.

"You fool!" Kakashi hollered, helpless to save him.

Naruto was just inches from the ground when Sasuke reached over to grab his ankle.

"Blockhead," Sasuke hissed, tightening his grip.

"Owww! That hurts!" Naruto howled.

At lunch that day, Kakashi made a major announcement.

"Your training is over," he told Naruto and Sasuke.

Kakashi had regained most of his strength, which meant Zabuza was probably better, too. No telling when they would see him again, but it could be any day now.

"Tomorrow we go back to guarding Tazuna," Kakashi said in a serious tone.

The bridge builder was surprised to hear the news.

"You still want to protect me? But I broke the contract."

"It's cowardly to see injustice and not act on it,"

Kakashi told him. "That's what our First Hokage always said. Ninja do not live by money alone."

Tazuna didn't reply, but his face shone with gratitude.

"How's the bridge coming along?" Kakashi asked. "I hear you're almost finished."

"We are!" Tazuna said happily. "That's why I'm covered in mud like a little kid!"

After lunch, Naruto and Sasuke returned to the forest to train until nightfall. When it was time to head back, Naruto was so exhausted he leaned on Sasuke for support.

By the time they got to Tazuna's, Naruto still felt like a limp rag. He wearily rested his head on the table as they waited for supper to be served. Soon he felt someone beside him.

He looked over to see Inari, his eyes full of tears.

"Why? Why?" Inari was sobbing.

The words tumbled out like a dam had burst.

"Why do you train so hard? You can't beat Gato! The bad guys always win!"

Naruto gave him a tired look.

"We're different from you," he muttered.

"You don't know anything about me!" Inari cried. "You don't know what it's like to suffer! All you care about is having fun!"

"Can I ask you something, Inari?" Naruto said quietly.

Inari glared back but didn't reply.

"Do you think it's okay to bawl all the time? To be the

star of your own little soap opera?"

Inari looked genuinely shocked, but Naruto had more to say.

"You know what you are, kid? A big fat crybaby!" he snapped. He kicked back his chair and left the room.

Inari looked stunned for a moment, then ran outside. He was sitting on the deck, gazing at the moon, when Kakashi gently approached him.

"Inari? Can I have a word with you?"

Inari didn't answer. Kakashi sat down beside him.

"He didn't mean to be cruel. Sometimes he just doesn't think."

Inari dabbed a tear from his eye.

"Let me tell you a little bit about Naruto," Kakashi said kindly.

As Inari gazed at the moon, Kakashi told him about a boy with no parents who had survived against the odds. A boy who kept on smiling no matter what life had handed him.

"Naruto just wants to be accepted," Kakashi explained. "He has risked everything to make that dream come true."

Inari didn't say anything.

"Naruto's done his share of crying, too. But he finally moved on. Going through all that has made him stronger, just like your father."

Inari swallowed hard.

"He picks on you for a reason, you know," Kakashi said

with a smile. "He thinks you two have a lot in common."

Kakashi kept smiling at him, but Inari still looked doubtful.

IN THE NICK OF TIME

Naruto didn't remember falling asleep that night. When he woke up the next morning, the sun was high in the sky and the house was quiet. Naruto couldn't even hear Tazuna, whose loud voice always bellowed over everyone else's.

"Agggh! I overslept!" Naruto spluttered.

He jumped out of bed and scooted to the living room in his pajamas. Tsunami sat on the floor, knitting, while Inari held her yarn.

"You up already, Naruto?" she said.

"Where is everybody?" Naruto asked breathlessly. "Sensei and Sasuke and Sakura..."

"At the bridge with my father. Kakashi said to let you sleep in since you looked so—"

Naruto didn't wait to hear the rest. Tsunami and Inari heard him clomping through the house as he got ready. Two minutes later he was back, dressed but still looking a little rumpled.

"See ya," he yelled, running out the door.

Naruto skipped the main road and entered the forest. The quickest way to the bridge was to travel through the trees. As he jumped from branch to branch, Naruto heard a rustling sound below him. He decided to go down and investigate.

Some of the plants on the forest floor had been roughly hacked away, scattering twigs and leaves and berries everywhere. The body of dead boar lay on a stump, completely cut to ribbons.

Somebody's been through here with a sword, he thought. *But who?*

Naruto looked more closely at the path of destruction. It seemed to lead right back to Tazuna's house.

He hesitated for a moment, worrying about what to do, then sped off down the trail of butchered greenery. It ended right where Naruto thought it would: Tazuna's.

Naruto could feel the bad vibes from where he stood. Someone evil was definitely inside.

But it doesn't feel like Zabuza, Naruto thought. In fact, the interloper's energy seemed fairly weak. But Tsunami and Inari could still be in danger.

"Hope I'm not too late!" he gulped, dashing to the door.

Inari was washing his hands in the bathroom when he

heard Tsunami scream.

"Mama!" he cried, running into the living room.

"Well! Who's this little darling?"

Two tall samurai sneered at Inari. One was shirtless and covered with tattoos, the other wore a winter coat and hat. They had slashed through a wall to get into the house.

Tsunami was cowering in a corner, looking desperately at her child.

"Should we grab him, too?" the tattooed one asked.

"One hostage is plenty," his cohort replied. "Kids are a pain to deal with later."

"Oh, well. Too bad for him!" the first one snorted, unsheathing his sword. Inari shook with terror.

"Touch one hair on his head and I'll bite my tongue off!" Tsunami shrieked.

The samurai glared at her. Tsunami glared back.

"You need a live hostage, right? If you hurt my son, you won't have one."

The samurai grimaced at each other. She did have a point. They needed to use her to get at Tazuna.

"Tsk! Okay, we'll leave him alone," the tattooed samurai sighed. He was just dying to cut someone up.

"Better thank your mommy, brat," said the other one. "She saved your little hide."

They tied Tsunami's hands behind her back and hustled her out the door.

Inari knelt on the floor, shaking and crying. If he had even tried to help his mama, the samurai would have killed him for sure. And Inari didn't want to die.

Then he remembered Naruto's words from last night.

You know what you are, kid? A big fat crybaby!

Inari flashed back to the day he had met Kaiza by the sea. Suddenly he understood what Kaiza had been trying to tell him.

If something is precious to you, you must protect it with your life! Even if you die...

Inari wiped away his tears and stood up like a man.

Can I be strong too, Daddy?

He dashed outside. The samurai were leading Tsunami away from the house.

"Wait!" Inari shouted.

They swung around to look.

"Not the brat again!" grumbled the guy with tattoos.

"Get away from my mama!" Inari cried, rushing at the samurai. They snickered and grabbed their swords.

"Inari!" Tsunami screamed.

The samurai quickly chopped Inari into pieces that fell to the deck with a clunking sound. But the pieces weren't Inari. They were heavy chunks of wood!

"What the—?" gasped one samurai.

"A Replacement Jutsu?" gasped the other.

Suddenly they heard a voice behind them.

"Sorry I'm late, guys! But heroes always arrive in the

nick of time!" someone yelled.

The samurai turned to see a blond kid hovering over the mother and son.

"Look! One of Tazuna's cut-rate bodyguards!" the tattooed guy snorted. They both started laughing.

Naruto ignored them and turned to Inari.

"Good job, buddy! When you distracted them, I was able to save your mama."

The samurai suddenly stopped laughing.

"You! You made fools of us!" they roared, marching toward Naruto with their swords.

"No sweat!" Naruto chuckled, winking at Inari. He tossed two shuriken at the samurai.

They easily knocked them down with their swords.

"Your little toys can't hurt us!" one sneered.

"Maybe not. But we can!" someone yelled behind their backs.

Two Naruto shadow clones fiercely kicked their heads. The samurai slammed to the deck, right on their ugly mugs. The impact left them both unconscious.

Naruto quickly tied them together from their ankles to their necks. Then he turned back to Inari.

"Sorry I called you a crybaby," Naruto said with feeling. "It's not true, okay?"

Inari looked at Naruto with wide eyes. Naruto patted him on the head.

"You're no crybaby, Inari. You're a big strong boy!"

Inari shut his eyes tight and scrunched up his face, but the tears still came pouring down.

"Aw, poop!" he said.

"What's wrong?"

"I don't wanna cry! You'll make fun of me again!" Inari whimpered, rubbing his eyes.

Naruto grinned.

"But, Inari! It's okay to cry when you're happy!"

They just looked at each other for moment, before Naruto had to hurry away.

"Gotta go! If they attacked here, the bridge will probably be a target, too."

Inari nodded.

"I'll leave the rest to you," Naruto said. "Heroes have

to help each other, right?"

"Right!" Inari yelled, punching his little fist in the air.

Little did Naruto know that the bridge had already been hit. Early that morning, while he was still asleep, the others had gone there to guard Tazuna. They weren't expecting any trouble, but they sure found it.

"Something feels wrong here," Sasuke said ominously.

"Yup," Kakashi agreed, looking around him.

"Look!" Sakura screamed, pointing in front of them. On the bridge lay five men in work clothes. Had they just collapsed—or were they dead?

Tazuna kneeled next to a man who showed some fleeting signs of life.

"What happened? Tell me!" Tazuna pleaded, cradling his head.

"M-monsters," the man said.

Kakashi looked up at the sky.

"I'll say this for Zabuza," he said dryly. "He has excellent timing."

All of a sudden, the clear blue sky turned dull and very gray.

"Here he comes!" Kakashi hollered.

Sasuke and Sakura leaped behind Kakashi and assumed their battle positions.

"This is his Hidden Mist Jutsu, right?" Sakura gasped.

Just then, a voice pierced through the fog.

"Kakashi! Long time, no see! Still babysitting the brats, eh?"

Sasuke shuddered from head to toe.

"Oh, dear! That little boy's trembling again, poor thing," Zabuza sneered.

Zabuza water clones popped up all around them. Sasuke was still shaking, but his face looked cool, calm, and very collected.

"Sure I'm trembling," he sneered back. "I'm trembling with anticipation."

Zabuza looked a little surprised.

"Okay, Sasuke! Go for it!" Kakashi yelled.

Sasuke dashed right through the water clones with amazing speed, leaving nothing behind but puddles. Then he took his place back in formation.

"So you saw through the water clones," Zabuza said. "You have a worthy rival, Haku."

A short distance away from them, Zabuza emerged from the mist. Behind him stood Haku, wearing his mask.

"So I was right," Kakashi said calmly. "That boy is in cahoots with Zabuza."

"He has some nerve!" Sakura snapped. "Showing up here after all he's done!" She took an angry step forward, but Sasuke stopped her.

"This one's mine," he said.

He stood very still and fixed his eyes on Haku.

"Quite a show you gave us, masked man," Sasuke

snapped. "You're an excellent actor. But you wanna know something? I *hate* actors."

"Sasuke is sooo cool!" Sakura sighed adoringly.

Kakashi glanced at her. If Naruto had said something like that, she would have bopped him in the head.

Haku looked over Sasuke with a critical eye.

"Impressive," he told Zabuza. "I know your water clones have only a tenth of your strength, but what he did was quite amazing."

"Enough babbling! Let's do it!" Zabuza growled.

"Yes, sir!"

Haku instantly spun away. Seconds later he showed up in front of Sasuke, looking like he didn't have a care in the world. Sasuke went at him with a kunai, but Haku stopped it with a senbon.

"I don't really want to kill you," he said quietly. "Why don't you just leave?"

"Don't be stupid," Sasuke said evenly. He looked just as calm as Haku.

"I was afraid you'd say that," Haku replied. "But you'll have a hard time keeping up with me. I've already set up my next two attacks."

"Next two attacks?" Sasuke gulped. A tiny trickle of sweat rolled down his forehead.

"First, we have water all around us. Second, your kunai is blocked by my senbon. You have only one hand free to defend yourself."

Haku also had only one free hand, but he immediately put it to good use. He started making signs, using a secret jutsu even Kakashi had never seen before.

"One-handed ninjutsu? Amazing!" Kakashi gasped.

"Secret Jutsu: A Thousand Needles of Death!" Haku announced when he finished.

He stamped his foot on the ground. The water instantly rose up in hundreds of long, sharp needles. Sasuke shut his eyes and focused all of his chakra on his feet.

Suddenly the water needles flew at Sasuke from every direction. Haku leaped out of the way.

But when the water splashed down again, Sasuke was gone. Haku looked around in shock.

Sasuke had used his chakra well. He knew the only escape route was right above his head. Seconds before the needles were about to hit, Sasuke soared to the sky like a firecracker.

Where is he? Haku wondered, looking around. He nearly missed the shuriken sailing toward his head, but jumped away just in time. When he landed, Haku heard a mocking voice behind him.

"You're pretty slow, masked man. Way slower than I thought you'd be."

Sasuke pointed his kunai at Haku's back. Haku stood like a statue, not saying a word.

"Better watch out. Now *I'm* running the show," Sasuke hissed.

Without warning, he attacked with his kunai. Haku managed to dodge every blow, but it wasn't easy.

He's fast! Haku thought, losing his balance.

Sasuke gave him a hefty kick right where it counted. Haku flew across the bridge and landed at Zabuza's feet.

"So. It wasn't just talk," Zabuza grunted.

"Don't sell us short," Kakashi said. "Sasuke is our number one rookie. And Sakura is our number one brain."

"Oh, really? What about that other kid, the blond twerp?" Zabuza scoffed.

"He's Naruto, our number one...ticking time bomb."

Zabuza looked amused.

"Hear that, Haku?" he sniggered. "We're in big trouble. If this goes on, they'll beat us at our own game."

Haku hesitated before he spoke.

"I'm really sorry about this," he said, looking down. He quickly made a sign, using both hands this time. An icy mist floated up from his body.

Where is all this cold air coming from? Sasuke wondered, bewildered. Then Haku chanted his jutsu.

"Secret Jutsu: Crystal Ice Mirrors!"

The water under Sasuke started to wriggle and squirm and dance up toward the sky. It hit the cold air and turned to crystals, forming thin ice walls that looked like mirrors.

As Kakashi and Sakura watched in horror, the walls encircled Sasuke, trapping him inside a very frosty jail.

Haku ran up and placed his palms on a wall. His body

was instantly sucked inside it.

Sasuke looked up in astonishment. Every icy mirror reflected an image of Haku.

"Blast!" Kakashi groaned, making a break for Sasuke. Zabuza quickly jumped in his path.

"This is our fight, remember?" he said menacingly. "Leave the boy to die."

Kakashi just stood there, grinding his teeth. One thing was bloody sure: he couldn't fight Zabuza and save Sasuke at the same time.

Inside the cold prison, Sasuke frantically looked around. Haku still gazed down at him from every mirror.

What's his next move? Sasuke wondered desperately. Then he heard Haku's voice.

"Now I'll show you some real speed."

Haku leaned out of a mirror and aimed his senbon. A sharp pain shot up Sasuke's arm.

In a flash, gusts of wind that felt like needles slashed through Sasuke's body. Everyone outside heard him scream in agony.

"Sasuke!" Sakura cried. She looked pleadingly at Tazuna, who nodded vigorously at her.

"It's okay! Go!" he said.

Sakura dashed up and hurled her kunai at one of the mirrors. Haku leaned out and caught it with one hand.

"Huh?" Sakura gasped, sweat dripping down her face.

Suddenly, a shuriken hit Haku's mask. He fell out of

the wall of ice and plopped to the ground with a thunk.

A cloud of flashy white smoke appeared at the end of the bridge. Sasuke was still sprawled on the ground, but he looked up to see who was coming.

"Show-off," he muttered, rolling his eyes.

Haku swung around to see. A small blond boy ran out of the smoke, looking quite heroic for someone so puny.

"I'm Naruto Uzumaki! Here to save the day!" he yelled.

Squad Seven's ticking time bomb had arrived.

DREAMS

"You all know how the story goes," Naruto sang out. "The hero arrives in the nick of time and turns the enemy into sashimi!"

Everybody gaped at Naruto, but each face showed a different emotion. Kakashi looked perplexed. Tazuna looked stunned. Sakura looked elated. Sasuke looked disgusted. And Haku? Impossible to tell with his mask on.

Only Zabuza looked unfazed. He seized the moment to quickly hurl five shuriken at Naruto.

Luckily, Naruto had still been on guard during his big hero act. He grabbed his kunai, but suddenly a senbon struck down every shuriken.

"Haku! What are you doing?" Zabuza barked.

Haku politely bowed to him.

"Sorry, sir. I want to fight him my way."

"Don't need my help, huh?" Zabuza grumbled, turning away. "Haku, you are innocent indeed."

Maybe Zabuza's right, Sasuke thought. *Maybe Haku is innocent.*

He inspected his wounds again. Scratches crisscrossed his body, but none of them were very deep. Haku could have easily killed him, but for some reason he chose not to. Suddenly Sasuke had a very grim notion.

Does he plan to torture me to death?

He looked at the mirrors of ice. Haku wasn't inside them now, but they were definitely the key to his attack. Sasuke was trying to figure out what to do next when Naruto noisily ran up.

"Yo, Sasuke! I'm here to rescue you!" he said excitedly.

"You doofus!" Sasuke snapped. "Now we're both screwed!"

They were both in Haku's trap, and Kakashi couldn't help them. He was still in a standoff with Zabuza.

"Hey! I went through heck to get here!" Naruto snapped back. "Can't you even say thanks?"

Suddenly Sasuke spotted Haku in a mirror.

That's him! The real him! he realized, grabbing his kunai. But before Sasuke could hurl it, he heard another voice in the background.

"Over here," Haku said.

Sasuke glanced back to see another Haku.

"Wh-what's goin' on here?" Naruto sputtered. Sasuke ignored him and quickly planned his next move.

These mirrors are made of ice, so...

Sasuke jumped up and made a sign.

"Fire Style: Fireball Jutsu!" he yelled.

It was the same jutsu Sasuke had used on Kakashi way back when, with one big difference. Now Sasuke knew how to control his chakra.

Red-hot fire roared out of his mouth, setting the ground ablaze. The flames flared up higher than the walls of ice. But when the fire subsided, the walls were still intact, as though nothing had happened.

Haku calmly gazed at Sasuke and Naruto from behind another mirror.

"It will take more than that to melt them," he said, raising his senbon.

Haku attacked again. In just seconds, Sasuke and Naruto were riddled with wounds. Sasuke writhed in pain, but Naruto had sustained less damage. He got up and gaped at the mirrors. Haku stared at him from every single one.

"Are they all clones?" Naruto yelled. "Where's the real guy?"

"Your eyes will never see the truth. You can never catch me," Haku said.

"Ha! We'll see about that!" Naruto snorted, quickly making signs.

Soon there was a Naruto clone for every Haku clone. The Narutos clenched their fists and charged.

"I'll punch out every one 'til I find the real guy!" Naruto vowed, aiming his fist at the closest mirror.

The clones instantly popped out of their mirrors and zipped right past Naruto's clones. The real Naruto was badly hurt, and fell to the ground with a thud.

"This jutsu uses the art of teleportation," Haku calmly explained. "I use the mirrors to hold my image. Then I can move faster than your eyes can follow."

Kakashi had been looking over Zabuza's shoulder, watching the fight.

"He's mastered *that* jutsu? At his age?" Kakashi gasped.

Zabuza just snickered.

"What jutsu?" Sakura asked nervously.

"It's a Kekkei Genkai," Kakashi told her. "Kekkei Genkai are genetic traits, like my sharingan. These jutsu are passed down from generation to generation by blood."

Sakura swallowed hard.

"But, sensei! Does that mean that—"

"Yes, Sakura. My sharingan can't copy that jutsu. There's nothing I can do."

Inside the ice walls, Naruto crouched next to Sasuke, looking almost totally wiped out.

"I've had enough," he mumbled.

"Do you give up, then?" Haku asked.

Naruto took a deep breath and struggled to his feet. Then he stubbornly glared at Haku.

"It can't end like this! I have a dream to fulfill!"

Haku flashed back to that day in the forest. Naruto had looked stubborn then, and he hadn't changed one bit.

But the sad thing was, Haku also had his dreams. As a little boy, he had been abandoned, unloved, thrown away. He had wandered aimlessly across the land, waiting to die.

One day a man saw Haku kneeling in the dust. He bent down to speak to him and got a funny feeling inside.

"I...I can see myself in your eyes," the man said.

That same man meant everything to Haku now.

He turned toward Sasuke and Naruto.

"I don't have the heart of a true shinobi," Haku confessed. "I don't really want to kill you. But if you come at me again, I will."

What's with this guy? thought Naruto and Sasuke. But Haku wasn't finished talking.

"You have your dreams, I have mine," he told them. "I have a special person in my life. My dream is to make his dream come true."

Haku gripped his senbon.

"If I have to become a true ninja to do that, I will—and kill you both."

Kakashi heard every word Haku said.

"They will never defeat a boy like him," he sighed.

"Wh-why not?" stammered Sakura.

Kakashi looked at her. Sakura was looking old before her time, and this was only her first assignment.

"He knows what it means to kill someone," Kakashi said grimly. "Naruto and Sasuke don't have the mental strength to take a human life yet."

Zabuza started to laugh.

"Har! You can't learn to be a ninja in a peaceful place like the Hidden Leaf Village!" he snorted. "A ninja needs to grow up with death nipping at his heels!"

Kakashi just glared at him.

"It's time to put an end to this," he muttered, reaching for his headband.

"Not the sharingan again!" Zabuza scoffed. "Is that the only trick you know?"

Zabuza lunged at Kakashi with a dagger he had hidden under his shirt. Kakashi blocked the blow meant for his heart with the palm of his right hand. Blood gushed out

dramatically, but Kakashi just smirked at his opponent.

"Just admit it, Zabuza! You're afraid of my sharingan! And you're terrified of me!"

"Tsk! Ninja shouldn't waste their secret weapons on any old foe!" Zabuza sneered.

"Lucky you, Zabuza! You get to see my sharingan twice! But trust me, there won't be a third performance."

"Go ahead and kill me!" Zabuza taunted. "But you'll never kill Haku."

He twisted the dagger in Kakashi's hand. More blood gushed out and dripped to the ground.

"I've been teaching him fighting skills since he was little," Zabuza said. "Now he's a perfect killing machine with a perfect secret weapon. A little thing called a Kekkei Genkai."

Zabuza pulled out the dagger and stepped back.

"Haku's better than the trash that tags behind you," he insisted.

"Sheesh! Is anything more boring than someone braggin' about his kid?" Kakashi grunted, pulling up his headband.

"Hold on! I'm not finished," Zabuza said quickly.

"Now what? You wanna show me his report card?"

"Heh, heh. Actually, you said a very funny line the last time we were together. I've been itching to say it back to you."

While Sakura and Tazuna watched anxiously from the

sidelines, Zabuza grinned merrily at Kakashi.

"I think it went something like this," Zabuza chortled. "'The same jutsu won't work on me twice.'"

Kakashi looked surprised. What was Zabuza up to now?

"Haku helped me figure out that magic eye of yours," Zabuza said. "And now I present—the Hidden Mist Jutsu!"

A heavy fog instantly spun around Zabuza until he was totally obscured from view. Then the fog drifted out to hide everything else.

"Sakura! Take care of Tazuna, okay?" Kakashi shouted through the mist.

"Okay, sensei!" Sakura shouted back.

Sakura dashed back to Tazuna and stood defensively, tightly gripping her kunai.

"Please don't move, Mr. Tazuna," she said firmly.

"All right, Sakura. But what kind of fog is this? I can barely see you."

Kakashi was bewildered, too.

"This fog is too thick for the Hidden Mist Jutsu. Not even Zabuza can see through it."

Holding a kunai in each hand, Kakashi repelled every single shuriken that flew out of the fog.

"Nice work," Zabuza snarled from behind. "That sharingan lets you dodge stuff you don't even see."

Kakashi swung around to face him. Zabuza's eyes were squeezed tightly shut.

Uh-oh! Kakashi thought with alarm. Zabuza faded behind the fog again, but he kept on talking.

"You pretend to see the future, but you're a total fraud. That sharingan is just a big old fake-out, designed to dupe your enemies."

Zabuza knew what he was talking about. Haku had studied Kakashi's sharingan and shared everything he learned. And Haku had learned a lot.

The sharingan is a jutsu that combines two amazing visual skills: the dosatsugan and the saimingan. Kakashi had used both to good advantage during his first match with Zabuza.

The dosatsugan (or Penetration Eye) allows the user to copy an enemy's physical movements. Kakashi had used his dosatsugan to copy Zabuza's every sign.

The saimingan (or Hypnosis Eye) is even more spectacular. It allows the user to copy an enemy's very thoughts. Kakashi knew what Zabuza would say before he even opened his mouth.

Both skills worked together to make Zabuza feel very vulnerable. After Zabuza totally lost his cool, Kakashi used visual hypnosis to trick him into doing his next jutsu. Then Kakashi copied it and went in for the kill.

"Now fighting you is a cinch," Zabuza boasted. "First, I just block your dosatsugan with fog and close my eyes. Then you can't hypnotize me *or* copy my jutsu!"

Kakashi sensed a shuriken flying toward his chest.

He managed to dodge it just in time, but the thick fog was really cramping his style.

"I can't see, but neither can you," Kakashi grunted.

"Ah, but you forgot something!" Zabuza chuckled.

"Forgot what?"

"That I'm a silent killing genius, silly! I can hunt by sound alone."

I can't believe this! Kakashi thought. *I fell right into his trap!*

He suddenly recalled the real reason that Zabuza was even here. It wasn't to kill Kakashi. He was doing a job for Gato.

Kakashi instantly jumped toward Tazuna and Sakura. Since he couldn't see, he had to rely on his memory of where they were standing.

Zabuza was already behind them, reaching for his sword. Sakura and Tazuna fearfully turned to look.

Just then, Kakashi jumped into the fray and pushed them both to safety.

"Too late!" Zabuza snorted.

"Sensei!" Sakura screamed.

Behind the ice mirrors, Sasuke and Naruto were still alive, though just barely. Naruto had collapsed on his stomach, looking like a porcupine with senbon quills. Sasuke crouched next to him, trying to catch his breath. Both of them were fading very fast.

They still couldn't see through Haku's jutsu, but they had managed to evade his worst blows. Now they were just waiting for a chance to fight back.

Sasuke had been backed into a corner, but for some reason he still felt calm.

This time, I'll see through him, he thought.

Sasuke stood up and glared at Haku. Then he focused all his senses on his enemy.

"You move well," Sasuke admitted. "But this is the end of you."

Haku instantly bombarded them with senbon. Sasuke saw them coming and dived out of the way, taking Naruto along with him. They slid across the icy floor until they finally came to a stop. Then Sasuke glared at Haku again.

Haku flinched when he saw his eyes.

He has the sharingan, too?

It was true. Both of Sasuke's irises had turned bright red, with black comma-shaped symbols within them.

"So you have a Kekkei Genkai, too," Haku calmly observed. "I'd better wrap this up quickly."

Haku was strong, but he knew his limits. His amazing jutsu used up large amounts of chakra. Haku could fight fast and furiously, but not for very long. Besides, Sasuke's two sharingan were already copying his movements. If the battle raged on, Haku would surely lose.

"This is it!" Haku yelled, jumping out of a mirror. Before, he seemed to move faster than the speed of light.

Now he looked almost slow to Sasuke.

Suddenly Haku lost all interest in killing Sasuke. He made a beeline for Naruto, who had collapsed in a heap on the ground.

Nooo! I have to get there first! Sasuke thought frantically.

Blood spurted from Kakashi's chest. Zabuza had wounded him deeply with his sword.

"You're slowing down, Kakashi," Zabuza snorted. "You know why? Your head's all wrapped up in trying to rescue those infants."

Kakashi gasped for breath as Zabuza kept on sneering.

"I wanna enjoy every minute of my victory. So forget about the brats, okay? Haku's already bumped them off."

"No way!" Sakura shrieked. "Sasuke won't give in to a kid like that! And neither will Naruto!"

"She's right," Kakashi said. "Naruto is a real tough cookie. And Sasuke is the sole surviving heir to the Hidden Leaf Village's most superior clan!"

That last sentence finally got Zabuza's attention.

"What? You mean—?" he gulped.

"Yup. He's Sasuke Uchiha. A true ninja genius, with a Kekkei Genkai to prove it."

Zabuza looked absolutely stunned for a second, but quickly recovered.

"Big deal! Haku is just as gifted!" he retorted. "And

no one has ever broken his secret jutsu." Then he ducked behind the fog again.

When Naruto finally came to, he saw Haku sprawled nearby, looking like his fighting days were over.

"Sheesh, Naruto," Sasuke muttered. "You're such a royal pain in the—"

"Sasuke! You did it!" Naruto yelled, turning in his direction. Then he gasped in horror.

Sasuke stood in a pool of blood, senbon all over his body. Though he could barely stand, he found the strength to glower at Naruto.

"Quit lookin' at me like that! Okay?"

All of a sudden, Naruto knew why he had survived. Sasuke had shielded him from senbon with his own body.

"Why, Sasuke? Why did you—" Naruto started to say, feeling agitated.

"How should I know?" Sasuke snapped back.

The truth was, during their long days of training, Sasuke had actually bonded with Naruto. But he would never, ever admit that to anyone.

"I used to hate you, you know," Sasuke grunted.

"So why did you rescue me then?" Naruto sputtered. "You should have minded your own business!"

Sasuke coughed up some thick blood.

"I dunno, okay?" he scowled. "My body just moved on its own."

Sasuke started falling backward. Naruto caught him just in time and gently lowered his body to the ground.

"I wanted to kill my brother before I died," Sasuke choked. "I thought that dream would keep me alive..."

What's wrong with him? He's so cold! Naruto thought.

"Don't you dare die, Naruto..." Sasuke gasped.

Then he closed his eyes.

Everything went deathly quiet. Finally Haku spoke.

"He struck one blow at me," he whispered. "Then he sacrificed himself for you."

Naruto looked up and saw Haku slowly rise to his feet.

"He knew it was a trap, yet he still saved someone special to him," Haku said. "He was a ninja to respect."

He entered another mirror, then looked down at Naruto.

"Is this the first time you've seen a comrade die? Such is a shinobi's path."

"Shut up," Naruto muttered. He was still cradling Sasuke's cold, lifeless body in his arms. A single tear rolled down his cheek.

I used to hate you, too. But I never wanted you to die.

A fierce anger welled up inside Naruto. Suddenly he looked at Haku with piercing eyes...the eyes of the demon fox.

"I'm gonna kill you!" he growled.

RETURN OF THE NINE-TAILED FOX

There was a dark feeling in the air.

Kakashi felt a chill up his spine and looked around for Zabuza.

"This isn't coming from him!" Kakashi suddenly realized. "This is coming from Naruto!"

That could only mean one thing. Naruto's seal was about to burst. The demon fox was about to break out. And Kakashi needed to do something, fast.

He grabbed a scroll from his pocket and rapidly unfurled it, then dipped his fingers in the deep wound on his hand. Kakashi drew a line on the scroll from end to end, using his own blood for ink.

"Enough screwing around, Zabuza!" Kakashi hollered, quickly re-rolling the scroll. "Let's end this right now!"

He held the scroll between his thumbs and furiously

made signs.

"Looks intriguing," Zabuza jeered. "Show me what you got."

Let me be in time! Kakashi desperately hoped. He tried to focus on the fight, but he kept worrying about Naruto.

Inside the prison of ice, Haku gaped at Naruto with shock. Visible swirls of chakra were rising up from Naruto's body. The senbon in his back all popped off and fell to the ground.

The swirls of chakra kept climbing to form the head of a giant fox. It glared at Haku with piercing eyes.

What kind of chakra is this? he thought. *It's hideous!*

While Haku watched in astonishment, Naruto's wounds rapidly healed. The fox made of chakra swirled back inside Naruto, but the freak show was far from over.

Naruto got down on all fours and growled like a wild animal. Then he glared at Haku with the same piercing eyes as the fox.

"Here he comes!" Haku gasped, grabbing his senbon.

Naruto bolted toward Haku with incredible speed.

"He's so bloodthirsty now!" Haku gulped. "What happened to the boy from the forest?"

He threw eight senbon at Naruto's head, in a move meant to kill him. Naruto opened his mouth and roared, sending the senbon right back where they came from!

He didn't even touch them! Haku thought. *His chakra repelled them!*

He jumped inside another mirror, too quickly for Naruto to notice. Naruto wildly looked around for his enemy. Haku hurled a senbon at his neck from above, but Naruto spun away.

Haku lost his target and his balance. He tried to jump inside another mirror, but his chakra was nearly gone. Naruto tore over to Haku and grabbed his wrist.

"Gaa-ooooooooo!" Naruto howled. The mirrors of ice started to crack. So did Haku's mask.

Is he a boy or a beast? he thought desperately, trying to break loose. Naruto aimed his fist at Haku's face.

Haku had never felt a punch like that. His whole body vibrated from the impact. A lesser shinobi would have died right there, but Haku was special. His light body flew through the air and fell to the ground with a thud.

Haku struggled to his feet. He had lost all will to fight.

Why am I getting up again? he wondered in a daze. Suddenly he remembered.

Zabuza. I have to win this for him.

Haku's mask was now so shattered, it barely held its shape. Naruto peered though the heavy fog and saw his enemy still standing.

"Gaa-ooooooooo!" Naruto howled again, zooming toward Haku with another fist filled with chakra.

All of a sudden, Haku's mask fell off. He had just one thought as he waited to die.

Sorry, Zabuza. This boy is better than me.

Naruto saw his face and skidded to a stop.

"It's you!" Naruto gasped. "The boy I met in the forest!"

"Why did you stop?" Haku asked. Naruto looked dumbfounded. Why would someone want to die?

"I killed your comrade!" Haku persisted. "Why don't you kill me?"

Naruto looked back at Sasuke, cold on the ground. His fist started to shake.

"Okay! I will!" Naruto shrieked, hitting Haku with all his might.

Haku landed on his hands and knees and coughed up a glob of dark blood. Then he glared at Naruto.

"Where did all your power go? A measly punch like that won't kill me," Haku grumbled.

But Naruto just kept thinking about what Haku had told him in the forest.

Is there someone special in your life? When people have someone special to protect, that often makes them stronger.

"Don't do me any favors," Haku said dully, wiping the blood from his mouth. "I'm ready to die now."

"Wh-what do you mean?" Naruto asked, looking intense.

"It would be too painful to live knowing I failed the man who meant most to me."

"But, but—" Naruto sputtered.

"Zabuza doesn't need a weak shinobi. You've taken

away my only reason for living."

Naruto gasped at Haku's shocking revelation.

The special person in his life...is Zabuza?

"You actually care about that creep with no eyebrows?" Naruto shrieked. "But he murders innocent men for money!"

Haku looked thoughtful before he finally replied.

"A long time ago, there were other special people in my life."

Naruto looked surprised.

"My parents," Haku said wistfully.

Naruto listened to every word as Haku told him the story of his life.

"I was born in a snowy little village in the Land of Mist," Haku said. "My parents loved me and loved each other, until...something happened."

He quickly looked at the ground.

"What? Tell me," Naruto pleaded.

"Blood," Haku said simply, wiping his mouth with the back of his hand. He looked down at the bright red stain and fell silent.

"Blood? What do you mean?" Naruto asked, confused.

"My father killed my mother, then tried to kill me."

"But wh-why?" Naruto shuddered.

"In the Land of Mist, anyone who had a Kekkei Genkai was considered a monster."

"Kekkei Genkai?"

"A special power that is only possessed by members of certain clans," Haku explained. "The people of the Land of Mist used our skills during wars. But eventually they stopped seeing us as warriors. Only as harbingers of doom."

Naruto listened to Haku with disbelief.

"When the wars were finally over, anyone with a Kekkei Genkai had to hide his true identity. If he didn't, he died."

Haku looked sadly at Sasuke's corpse.

"A Kekkei Genkai is a mixed blessing, as your comrade must have known. We are special. We are powerful. And we are feared."

Naruto had never known just why Sasuke was special. But he didn't doubt what Haku was saying.

"My mother had a Kekkei Genkai, but she never told my father. When he found out, he killed her. And before I knew what I was doing..."

Haku got a faraway look in his eyes.

"...I killed him."

Naruto felt his throat tighten. He'd been through a lot in his young life, but nothing compared to this.

"The most painful thing for me was accepting the truth," Haku said quietly.

"What truth?" Naruto asked.

"That I was completely, utterly alone. No one cared if I lived or died."

I used to feel that way, Naruto remembered sadly.

Haku looked up at Naruto.

"Remember that day in the forest? You said you wanted to be the best ninja in your village, so everyone would respect you."

"What does that have to do with this?" Naruto asked.

"If someone respects you like that, they become special to you. For me, that person was Zabuza."

Haku started to cry.

"I was so happy," he said tearfully. "Zabuza knew my secret, yet he still valued me. Nobody else did."

He smiled faintly, remembering the fateful day they met.

It was true, Zabuza had accepted the little boy nobody wanted. For the first time in ages, Haku actually felt hopeful. Then Zabuza broke the bad news—he had to leave the Land of Mist.

"But I'll be back someday," Zabuza vowed. "And crush them all under my feet!"

He suddenly looked down at little Haku.

"I don't need love, or affection, or support from you. What I need is—"

The little boy smiled up at his rescuer.

"I understand, Zabuza," he said. "Let me be your weapon. Keep me beside you and I'll always obey."

Zabuza beamed down at him.

"Good boy," he said.

From that day forward, Haku had given his all to Zabuza. His amazing skills made impossible assignments seem effortless. Haku vowed he would keep on fighting until Zabuza's dream came true.

But now, in Naruto, Haku had finally met his match. In his mind, there was only one solution.

"Please, Naruto. Kill me."

Kakashi held the scroll as he kept making signs. Then he kneeled and pushed it into the dirt.

"Summoning, Earth Style: Fanged Pursuit Jutsu!!" Kakashi hollered.

Zabuza was quickly losing patience with him.

"Enough of this magic act, Kakashi!" he groused. "You can't see me, but I can clearly see you. And you're right where I want you to be."

Zabuza felt so confident he closed his eyes again. Just then the earth rumbled loudly beneath his feet. Zabuza opened his eyes and looked down with fright.

"Noooo!!!" he gasped.

A pack of mad dogs suddenly broke through the ground, scattering big clods of dirt everywhere. Each one wore a Leaf headband around its neck like a collar. The dogs were of different breeds, but they shared one thing in common. They all looked at Zabuza like he was a piece of raw meat.

"Aaaaagh!!!" Zabuza yelled, as they went for him.

He couldn't run away. Two dogs had already sunk their fangs in his ankles. The other dogs quickly sunk their fangs in the rest of him.

Kakashi slowly emerged from the fog.

"That's why I let you hurt me," he explained. "My blood is smeared all over your sword. My little ninja puppies picked up the scent!"

Zabuza just glared at him, as blood and dog spit trickled down his body.

"Now you're right where *I* want *you* to be," Kakashi said with satisfaction.

Zabuza angrily tried to pull away from the dogs, but they refused to let him go.

"The mist is gone, Zabuza. I can see your future again," Kakashi said grimly.

"Yeah? I've heard enough of your bluffs," Zabuza snorted.

"Who's bluffing now?" Kakashi scoffed. "Give up, Zabuza. There's nothing you can do but die."

Kakashi walked up and looked straight into Zabuza's demon eyes.

"You got too greedy, Zabuza."

Kakashi was right. The sorry tale of Zabuza Momochi had spread through every shinobi village. He was the guy who tried to assassinate the Mizukage of the Hidden Mist Village. When he failed, he dropped out of sight. Since then, Zabuza had worked for worms like Gato to raise money for a future comeback.

Kakashi laced his fingers together and clasped his hands, then focused all of his chakra into his right palm.

"I'm not just about the sharingan, you know," Kakashi said. "You will now witness the only original jutsu of Kakashi, the famous copy ninja."

With a thunderous boom, a lightning bolt zapped out of his right palm.

"Lightning Blade!" Kakashi yelled.

"What the—??" Zabuza gasped. "I can almost see the chakra in his hand!"

Kakashi kept talking while his palm sizzled and hissed.

"Your greed claims too many victims. That is not the path of a true shinobi."

"I don't care!" Zabuza snapped. "I fight for what I believe in, and I'm not about to stop."

Kakashi had only one thing left to say to him.

"Give up—or your future is death."

"What are you waiting for, Naruto?" Haku said tiredly. "Please kill me now."

Sweat rolled down Naruto's face as he stared at Haku. How could he look so peaceful?

"I don't get it!" Naruto yelled. "You wanna die just because someone defeated you?"

Haku didn't answer.

"You're more than just a fighter," Naruto argued. "Your boss must know that."

Haku laughed sadly.

"When we met you in the forest, I remember thinking we were two of a kind. Surely you can understand."

Haku stood very still and closed his eyes. He lifted his chest a little to make an easier target for Naruto.

"Sorry you have to dirty your hands with this," he said quietly. "But I hope your dream comes true."

The boy who stood in front of him had killed his comrade in cold blood. Naruto looked at Sasuke's body.

"He had a dream, too," Naruto whispered.

He pulled a kunai from his leg holster. Naruto moved slowly at first, then quickened his pace. Soon he was zooming toward Haku, a kunai aimed straight at his heart.

Haku calmly accepted his fate. If that boy killed him, then so be it. Naruto was simply stronger than he was.

But just as the kunai was about to pierce his chest, Haku grabbed Naruto's wrist.

"Huh?" Naruto gasped.

"I'm sorry, Naruto," Haku said. "But I can't die yet."

He made a sign and disappeared, leaving behind a curling wisp of cold air.

Kakashi thrust out his hand and raced toward Zabuza. A crackling sound echoed through the fog. Zabuza was still covered with dogs, so all he could do was gape in astonishment.

All of a sudden, another ice wall appeared behind Zabuza. Kakashi looked surprised, but he didn't slow down.

When Kakashi reached Zabuza, his fingernails turned into blades. They ripped through Zabuza's flesh and shredded his bones into splinters. That should have been the end of him...

But then the dogs vanished in a cloud of smoke. Kakashi quickly looked down at the scroll of summoning. Five senbon were stabbed right through it. The ice wall behind Zabuza shattered to the ground.

Kakashi looked up again and gasped.

Haku stood mutely before him, drenched in blood. He had taken the attack meant for Zabuza.

He grabbed Kakashi with a shaky hand.

"Zabuza..." Haku choked.

Meanwhile, on another part of the bridge, Naruto was still looking for Haku. When the fog finally cleared, Naruto thought he saw him in the distance. But what was he doing to Kakashi?

Naruto dashed toward them. When he saw Haku, he gasped.

"Wh-what's going on!?" he screamed. Nobody but Zabuza spoke.

"That was brilliant, Haku!" he said, hoisting his sword.

Kakashi tried to pry himself away from Haku, and had a sudden, grisly realization.

The boy was dead. And Zabuza was going to hack right through him to get to Kakashi.

"What a treasure I found way back when!" Zabuza rejoiced, swinging his blade. "In the end, he gave me the perfect gift!"

With Haku's corpse still clinging to him, Kakashi used all his strength to jump back. He landed a short distance away and carefully laid the body on the ground. Then he knelt down and gently pulled the lids over Haku's eyes.

"Heh, heh. You only got away because Haku's dead," Zabuza jeered.

Naruto shook with rage at Zabuza's heartlessness.

"Stay back, Naruto," Kakashi warned, keeping his eyes on Zabuza. "This is my fight."

As Naruto nodded reluctantly, Sakura ran up with Tazuna.

"Naruto! You're alive!" she cried with relief.

Naruto gaped at Sakura with wide eyes.

"But what about Sasuke? Where's Sasuke?" Sakura exclaimed, looking behind Naruto.

Naruto kept gaping at her, then quickly looked away. He didn't have to say a word. Sakura knew from the look on his face that something horrible had happened.

"Focus, Kakashi!" Zabuza roared, wielding his long sword. "Forget about the brats!"

And so the fight continued.

THE DEATH OF
A DANGEROUS MAN

Sakura kneeled down and put her hand on Sasuke's cheek.

"He's so...cold," she whispered. "This isn't just an illusion. It's...real."

"Sakura..." Tazuna said gently. She looked so young and so small to him now.

"Go ahead and cry. Just pretend I'm not even here."

Tears flooded Sakura's eyes as she struggled to speak.

"Wh-when I was at the academy, I aced every test. I memorized the Rules of Conduct, every one of them."

Tazuna noticed Sakura was trembling all over.

"One day the sensei asked us about Rule 25. I wrote down the answer just like always.

"'A ninja must never show emotion, no matter what

happens!'" Sakura sobbed. "'The assignment always comes first. And never, ever shed a tear.'"

So this is a ninja's life, Tazuna thought sadly.

Naruto was thinking the very same thing as the battle moved toward its bloody finale.

"Why can't I catch up?" Zabuza choked, gasping for breath. He still carried his sword, but the handle was smeared with his blood. His wounded left arm drooped limply by his side.

"Agggggh!" Zabuza groaned. He dashed forward with all the fighting spirit he could muster, but Kakashi easily swatted him away. Zabuza wildly swung his sword, but Kakashi was already gone.

Suddenly Zabuza felt a hand on the back of his neck.

"You can never beat me now," Kakashi said.

"What?" Zabuza gasped.

"It's over. You just haven't realized it yet," Kakashi said. He held two kunai together and swung them at Zabuza.

"This is goodbye, demon..."

Zabuza pulled back his sword and twisted his body. The kunai missed his vital organs and slashed his right arm.

Kakashi stumbled backward and fell on his side, but quickly pulled himself up. Zabuza looked helplessly at his two mangled arms.

"How will you do jutsu now?" Kakashi sneered.

"Well, Zabuza! He certainly made a mess out of you!" a familiar voice sneered.

Zabuza raised his bloody face to look.

"Gato..."

The most hated man in the Land of Waves was approaching from beyond the bridge. He didn't come alone. A small army of samurai were with him.

Kakashi glared at Gato with angry eyes. This short, ugly man was to blame for all this suffering.

"What are you doing here?" Zabuza growled. "And why did you bring them?"

"There's been a change of plans, Zabuza," Gato snickered. "Your plans. Get ready to bite the dust, demon."

"What?" Zabuza gasped.

"I never intended to pay you," Gato said. "That's why I hire rogue ninja. No one complains if I kill them at the end of a job. So I get all my work done for free!"

Zabuza growled behind his mask.

"You're no demon, Zabuza!" Gato scoffed. "Just a little baby devil."

He threw back his head and laughed. The samurai joined in, hooting and hollering and stomping their feet. Zabuza didn't scare them one bit. There was only one of him, after all, and lots and lots of them.

Zabuza turned to Kakashi.

"Forgive me, Kakashi. I have no reason to kill Tazuna now. This fight is officially over," he said soberly.

"Agreed," Kakashi nodded, keeping his eyes on Gato and his men.

Suddenly Gato saw Haku on the ground nearby. He rushed up and cruelly kicked his corpse.

"That brat broke my wrist!" he spit out. "Now he's dead, and good riddance!"

Naruto glowered at Gato.

"Leave him alone, you creep!" he shrieked, galloping toward him. Kakashi quickly grabbed the back of his jumpsuit.

"Just calm down, Naruto," he warned. "There are way too many of them."

While Kakashi held him back, Naruto yelled at Zabuza.

"Why are you just standing there? You meant everything to him! Didn't he mean anything to you?"

"Shut up, kid. Haku is dead."

"But that scumbag stepped on his face! Don't you even care?" Naruto snapped.

"Gato used me, and I used Haku," Zabuza muttered. "There are just two kinds of ninja, you know. Ninja who use people, and ninja who get used."

Zabuza gazed into the distance for a moment.

"I didn't want Haku for himself," he finally said. "I only wanted his skills. I have no regrets whatsoever."

"Do you...do you really mean that?" Naruto asked with astonishment.

"Let it go, Naruto," Kakashi said firmly. "This fight is over. Besides, we have to—"

Naruto wriggled away from Kakashi.

"Shut up! He's still my enemy!" he shouted.

Zabuza just looked at the ground. He was having a hard time facing Naruto. Kakashi had nothing to say, either. But Naruto refused to let the matter drop.

"He cared about you!" Naruto yelled, pointing at Haku. "Don't you feel anything for him?"

Haku had lost more than a battle. He had lost his whole reason for living. How could Zabuza be so heartless? Was that why they called him a demon?

"He gave his life for you!" Naruto cried, tears streaming down his face. "He never even had his own dream! All he cared about was your dream!"

"Kid," Zabuza muttered.

"That's terrible!" Naruto choked.

"Kid," Zabuza muttered, louder this time.

Naruto looked up with surprise. Zabuza's eyes were glistening with tears.

"Not another word," he whispered. He looked away for a long moment, then turned back to Naruto.

"Haku was too kind," Zabuza mumbled. "He never truly wanted to kill anybody."

Zabuza ripped off his tattered mask before he went on.

"I'm glad my last battle was against you," he told Naruto. "And you're right, you know."

"Huh?" Naruto said.

"We ninja are still just people after all, with the same feelings as anyone..."

Zabuza sighed.

"Now I've lost everything," he said quietly. There were no more tears in his eyes. In fact, Zabuza looked almost peaceful, as if he had finally accepted his fate.

But he still wasn't ready to walk away.

"Can I borrow your kunai, kid?" he suddenly asked.

"Sure," Naruto said, tossing it to him. Zabuza caught it in his mouth and ran toward Gato.

"Kill him!" Gato screamed. "Kill all of them!"

The samurai excitedly raised their weapons and rushed forward, ready to show their stuff.

Then they saw Zabuza. The giant head of an angry beast swirled in the air behind him.

"It's a demon!" the samurai gasped.

They pierced Zabuza with so many weapons he looked like a pincushion, but he still didn't fall.

Gato gaped with shock as Zabuza tore through his army, samurai by samurai. Soon Zabuza was standing right in front of him, the kunai still in his mouth.

Zabuza grinned as he stabbed Gato in the gut. Three samurai instantly thrust spears into his back, but Zabuza still didn't go down.

"Why won't you die?" a samurai wailed.

"You want to join your little friend? Then go there alone!" Gato choked, blood streaming from his mouth.

"I won't be allowed to go to the same place as Haku," Zabuza said calmly.

"Wh-what are you babbling about?" Gato stuttered.

"I'm going to a hotter place—and I'm taking you with me!" Zabuza roared.

He yanked his kunai out of Gato. More blood spurted from his gut.

"When we get there, then you'll see who's a little baby devil!" Zabuza hollered, lunging at Gato's neck.

Gato's severed head flew up like a comet with a bloody tail. Then it fell to earth and rolled toward the samurai, who shrieked in horror.

Zabuza glared at them with demon eyes as he stood beside Gato's body. The kunai that had killed their kingpin was clenched between his teeth. The samurai shrieked again.

Suddenly the kunai fell from Zabuza's mouth. As he crumbled to the ground, Zabuza remembered what Haku had told him the day they met.

Keep me beside you and I'll always obey...

"Goodbye, Haku," he whispered. "Thanks for everything..."

Naruto gulped and looked down at his feet.

"Don't look away, Naruto," Kakashi said quietly. "This is the last moment of a man who lived dangerously."

Naruto nodded. He knew Zabuza had been a bad man, but his heart still ached for him.

EPILOGUE

Am I dead? Sasuke thought. *Where am I?*

All he could see was darkness.

Was that a sound in the distance?

Sasuke strained to hear.

"Sasuke...Sasuke..." someone was sobbing.

It sounded like Sakura. But why in the world was she crying?

"Sasuke...Sasuke..."

"Sakura..."

Sasuke felt something heavy on his chest and slowly opened his eyes. Sakura was sprawled across him, weeping uncontrollably.

"Uh, Sakura? You're hurting me," Sasuke murmured.

Sakura jolted upright, her eyes brimming with tears.

"Sasuke! Oh, Sasuke!" she cried.

Sasuke looked behind Sakura. Tazuna was beaming at them both.

Sasuke slowly got to his knees and tried to recall what had happened. The last thing he remembered was shielding Naruto from Haku's attack.

"Sakura, how's Naruto? And that scumbag in the mask?"

"Naruto's okay. But the boy in the mask is dead."

"Dead?" Sasuke gasped. "Did Naruto—?"

Sakura shook her head.

"I think he died trying to save Zabuza."

"Oh."

So he never intended to kill us, Sasuke thought.

"Naruto! Sasuke's alive!" Sakura shouted.

Naruto heard her and swung around. Sasuke was on his feet now. He didn't look at Naruto, but he did raise his hand a little. Not exactly a wave, but coming from Sasuke, it almost counted as a hug.

Naruto looked at Haku's lifeless body and had the same thought as Sasuke.

He never intended to kill us. Goodbye, Haku...

"Sasuke's okay? Great!" Kakashi said.

"Hey, ninja! This ain't over!" somebody hollered.

Zabuza had killed quite a few samurai, but there were plenty left, and they were all in a nasty mood.

"You jerks murdered our meal ticket!" a samurai yelled. "And now you're gonna die!"

"Then we'll sack this village for valuables!" yelled another.

"Yeah!" yelled the rest.

They raised their weapons and charged.

"Hoo-boy," Kakashi groaned. "This can't be good."

Naruto looked at him in desperation.

"Sensei! Is there a jutsu that can flatten 'em all at once?" he asked hopefully.

"Naruto!" Kakashi gasped. "Just how much chakra do you think I have left?"

Suddenly a long harpoon flew through the air and landed among the samurai.

"Hey! What's this?" they shrieked.

Everybody swung around to look. A mighty mob of villagers were swarming over the bridge, armed with spears and shovels and anything they could find.

A tiny boy marched in front, carrying a small crossbow. He wore a rice pot for a helmet and a frying pan strapped to his back.

"I-Inari?" Tazuna gasped.

"Inari!" Naruto yelled.

The villagers raised a battle cry.

"Go back where you came from—or die!" they yelled in unison. Tazuna was absolutely stunned.

"You...You all came," he gasped, looking at the crowd. He saw neighbors and friends and fellow laborers who had helped him with the bridge. Even his old friend Giichi had joined the fight. Gato's gang didn't scare him anymore.

Tears streamed from Tazuna's eyes, and he didn't even

try to hide them. The villagers were finally sticking up for themselves. But what had caused this sudden change of heart?

One small boy in an upside-down flowerpot hat. Naruto's courage had inspired Inari to go door to door and rally the troops.

"We need to get to the bridge!" Inari had pleaded. "We can beat Gato and his gang together."

The villagers were wary at first.

"Sorry, Inari, but I don't want to fight back," Giichi had told him. "I've lost too much to Gato already."

"So have I," Inari said stubbornly. "That's why I have to fight."

Something about Inari had touched the heart of every villager. He had looked so sad, so helpless, after Kaiza died. Now here he was, outside their doors, looking as strong and determined as his father. Could the impossible become possible again?

The villagers decided to find out. Now the sad little boy was beaming as he led them across the bridge.

"Hey, Naruto!" Inari yelled. "A hero shows up in the nick of time, right?"

"Right! I'll help you, too!" Naruto yelled back, making a sign.

Naruto's chakra was almost on empty, but he managed to make a few clones. The samurai looked at them nervously, which gave Kakashi a bright idea.

"I can't do much," he said tiredly, making a sign. "But I can at least do something." A gang of Kakashi clones suddenly showed up, ready for action.

Luckily, they didn't have to lift a pinkie. The samurai squealed like little girls and scurried back to their ship.

"It's over!" the villagers cried out with joy.

"Yeah," Zabuza said weakly. Kakashi looked down at him. Though Zabuza was close to death, his flames of life were still flickering.

He must have unfinished business, Kakashi thought.

"I have a favor to ask," Zabuza said with difficulty. "Can I...Can I see his face?"

Kakashi kneeled down and gently pulled the spears from Zabuza's body. Then he carefully lifted him up.

All of a sudden, soft white flakes started drifting down from the sky.

"Snow?" Naruto gasped. "But it's almost summer!"

Are you crying, Haku? Zabuza thought.

Kakashi laid him next to Haku, then quietly walked away.

"Kakashi...thank you," Zabuza said in a hushed tone.

Using every ounce of strength he had left, he turned to look at Haku.

"You were always by my side," Zabuza whispered. "I want to die by your side." He put his hand on Haku's cheek.

"I...I just wish we were going to the same place..."

Snowflakes fell on Haku's face, then melted and flowed like tears.

Naruto watched from nearby, bawling uncontrollably.

"Haku's v-village was v-very snowy," he sobbed.

"That boy had a pure spirit," Kakashi said quietly. "As pure and clean as freshly fallen snow."

As he watched Zabuza's life ebb away, Kakashi had one last thought.

You can go with him, Zabuza. You can go to that place together...

Two weeks passed.

Tazuna's bridge was finished at last. And with no Gato around, the village was slowly coming to life again. Soon the day came for the ninja of the Hidden Leaf Village to finally go home.

They visited the graves of Zabuza and Haku to bid a final goodbye. Two wooden posts stood side by side. Haku's long sash was tied around his marker. Behind Zabuza's stood his giant sword. There were also garlands of flowers and plates of rice cakes, offerings for the gods.

Naruto hungrily reached for a rice cake when he thought no one was looking. Sakura slapped his hand.

"You can't eat that!" she snapped. "The gods will punish you!"

Naruto blushed sheepishly.

Sakura then turned to Kakashi with a worried look on

her face.

"Sensei? Is it true what they said about ninja?" she asked in a small voice.

"Yes," Kakashi said, gazing soberly at the graves.

"We ninja are really just instruments," he went on. "We go wherever we're needed, without worrying about why we exist."

"That's what it means to be a real ninja?" Naruto griped. "I don't like the sound of that!"

"Do you feel that way, Kakashi-sensei?" Sasuke asked earnestly. Kakashi shook his head.

"Not really. But every ninja tries to live up to that ideal. Even Zabuza and Haku."

Naruto had been looking sadly at the graves. Suddenly he clenched his fists.

"I've made up my mind," he said. "I'll follow the way of the ninja—but in my own way."

Kakashi looked at his charges. Squad Seven's first assignment had made them grow up more than he ever dreamed they would.

And Kakashi was very proud.

Tazuna, Tsunami, and Inari sadly watched their friends walk away. Tears flowed down Inari's cheeks, but he didn't even care. It was okay to cry sometimes. Naruto had taught him that.

"You finally built your bridge, Father," Tsunami said wistfully.

"I didn't build that bridge. Naruto did," Tazuna replied. They started walking back to the house on the sea.

"You know, the bridge still needs a name," Tazuna said thoughtfully. "But only one seems truly right."

"What's that, Grandpa?" Inari piped up.

"How about the Great Naruto Bridge?"

For years to come, strangers often asked about the bridge when they visited the Land of Waves.

The villagers would tell them about the brave band of ninja who had saved their town and their spirits.

"Who is the bridge named for?" the strangers would wonder.

The villagers always grinned before they answered.

"It's named for a hero!" they proudly replied.

"A hero named Naruto!"